SMALL BUSINESS TAX SAVINGS HANDBOOK

TRIO HILL PUBLISHING

Published by Trio Hill Publishing
Milwaukee, Wisconsin
www.TrioHill.com

ISBN: 979-8-9918685-0-1 (Paperback)
ISBN: 979-8-9918685-1-8 (eBook)
Library of Congress Control Number (LCCN): 2024922909

This book is a work of nonfiction. The content is intended for general informational purposes and does not constitute specific tax, legal, or accounting advice. While the publisher and author have made every effort to ensure accuracy as of the publication date, tax laws change frequently, and the strategies discussed may not apply universally. Neither the publisher nor the author assumes liability for damages arising from the use of this material.

Readers are advised to consult a qualified tax professional before making any decisions based on the information in this book. Not all strategies discussed may be suitable for every individual or business, and there is no guarantee of actual tax savings.

By using this book's content, you acknowledge that you bear full responsibility for your financial decisions and that neither the author nor publisher provides specific legal, financial, or tax advice.

Printed in the United States of America

10 9 8 7 6 5 4 3 2 1

SMALL BUSINESS TAX SAVINGS HANDBOOK

How to Save on Taxes While Growing Your Business and Wealth

MIKE JESOWSHEK, CPA

TRIO HILL
PUBLISHING

CONTENTS

INTRODUCTION

By picking up this book, you're taking a major step in your entrepreneurial journey. And just because you're here to learn more about tax planning, you're already way ahead of the curve.

Why? Tax planning is a vital part of growing both your business and your wealth. When they hear "tax," most business owners immediately think about filing their taxes. Very few initially consider tax *planning*. And this is an enormous missed opportunity.

Don't get me wrong, tax filing is important—so important it's legally required, and you get to do it every year. But the process of filing your taxes is pretty straightforward. It's just taking the information you already have at the end of the year and sending it to the state and federal government. It comes down to checking off boxes and filling in blanks.

But tax planning is much different. It's something you do throughout the year, not just once a year, and you do it because it can save you money and make your life easier. Learning and implementing tax strategies consistently is essential.

You'll notice I said learning *and* implementing—both are essential. You'll keep learning new tax strategies for the rest of your life, and you should be implementing what you're learning as you go. Being proactive, not just doing things the way you've always done them, is what produces results.

Before we dive into tax-saving strategies that I know will work for you, let me share my story and explain why you can trust this advice.

My Story

My name's Mike, and I am the host of the Small Business Tax Savings Podcast and the founder of TaxElm. Here is my backstory.

I started my entrepreneurial journey at a young age. When I was around eight or nine, I often attended auctions with my dad. He owned an antique store and was constantly on the hunt for new finds to sell. As a kid, I appreciated drinking root beer and playing pool in the back more than watching adults quietly compete to buy dusty-looking objects and trinkets.

Needless to say, I wasn't very involved with anything my dad did or bought at these events, except for one particular purchase. It was a box of a couple of thousand bottle caps from some old soda. My dad got it for just $20 or $30 and made it my project. I was instructed to divide these bottle caps into groups of 50 and put them into sandwich bags.

Then, we went to eBay and sold the individual bags for over $50 each. Remember, we bought thousands for no more than $30, and each bag sold for more than that. As you can imagine, this made the hobby *much* more interesting for me. I'd say this is where my entrepreneurial spirit was born and one of my first memorable experiences making money.

MY FIRST BUSINESS

After that, I was all in. I started my first business at the age of fourteen. It was an online marketing company, and I rewarded people for signing up for different services. If a company was trying to grow its customer base, I'd find interested consumers and offer them incentives to sign up. I also created and sold e-books. I'd write e-books about various topics, like "How To Create Your Own Corn Hole Game," and sell them on eBay. These provided a steady source of passive income. I exited the business at eighteen for a whopping $7,000. I still have the purchase agreement on my wall. I was ecstatic—on top of the world.

Then, it was time for the next chapter. I wanted to continue with online marketing but decided to go to college for accounting as a backup plan. As a student, I worked toward an accounting degree while exploring various business opportunities. I owned a few businesses and co-owned a few more. I experienced both massive successes and failures, along with a range of valuable lessons in between. I learned a lot about the stages of the business life cycle firsthand and earned a decent income.

And as you well know, income leads to a tax bill. I knew a bit about taxes but thought my income was too low to benefit from tax-saving strategies. Tax-saving strategies were for people who made a lot more than me, and I had to suck it up until I was wealthier. Because you have to be rich to qualify for tax breaks, right?

Wrong—and that's a mistake I don't want you to make. This book will show you how anyone, regardless of income, can benefit from tax planning.

THE BACKUP PLAN

In 2011, I partnered with six others to create an online marketing company. At this point, I got deeper into the accounting side of the business, and I loved it. Each partner was highly talented in different areas of the industry. Instead of trying to pull the company into multiple specialties, we decided to split the work so all of us could focus on what we do best.

This endeavor inspired me to start a digital accounting firm in 2013. The online marketing industry showed me an entirely different side of accounting and introduced me to a niche where everyone worked virtually. Now, virtual work is common. Then, it was novel. I decided to explore opportunities in virtual accounting for online marketing firms. It worked to my benefit that I already had a good reputation in the industry and plenty of specialized experience, and it didn't take long to build a roster of clients. We offered bookkeeping services in-house and outsourced tax work.

Naturally, clients always came to me with tax questions, and I'd ask around with other accountants I worked with for help answering them. I quickly realized that no one gives a straight answer to these things.

> *How can my client hire their kids?*
> It depends...
>
> *Does this client qualify for the home office deduction?*
> It depends...
>
> *What is the right way for my clients to pay themselves?*
> It depends...

This type of runaround was incredibly frustrating to me. I *knew* there were variables involved and that the same solutions wouldn't apply to everyone, but I wanted answers.

So, I started researching and found that I couldn't stop at "yes" or "no." I needed to know *why* something applied or didn't apply, *how* best to classify expenses and find breaks, *when* it made sense to use different strategies, and *what* options people had to save money.

I became obsessed with helping my clients pay the least amount in taxes legally possible.

I wanted to show people that doing things a little differently with their business bookkeeping could make a lot of difference in their taxes. ***This* is what I mean by "tax planning."** It's not just preparing for that tax return but molding the financial choices you make year-round to serve your business best now and in the future.

Realizing this gave me the idea for this book and my other programs. On top of my prior experience running a full-service accounting firm, I:

- Host the Small Business Tax Savings Podcast every week.
- Offer training programs for minimizing taxes.
- Publish regular posts about all things tax-related.
- Moderate online groups where business owners can share ideas and stories.
- Built software to help business owners understand what strategies are relevant to them and exactly how to implement them (TaxElm).
- Speak at various conferences and appear as a guest on podcasts across the country.

I can't get enough of this. Teaching savvy entrepreneurs to be more tax-smart is my passion, and I'm determined to find every way possible to reach people with these resources.

I aim for every business owner to know the strategies available to them inside and out to pay the smallest tax bill possible. And now, that includes you.

Your Story

By the end of this book, you'll walk away with your success story.

This book is written specifically for small business owners and aspiring entrepreneurs like you. If you own a billion-dollar company, this book may not be a perfect fit—but even then, you will pick up helpful strategies.

I'll give you easy-to-understand, to-the-point information and strategies you can implement in your business now. I *won't* beat around the bush or give half-answers.

With that said, how you should plan ultimately *does* depend. Everyone's situation is different, and you might need to tweak strategies to make them work for you. My goal is to get you at least 90% to 95% of the way there with general advice. For the last 5% to 10%, you'll need to make slight changes based on your situation. I recommend talking to your accountant about what you learn here or doing follow-up research to finalize your game plan.

The *concept* of a tax strategy is the same for everyone, and I will give you the tools you need to start planning.

When I talk about tax planning, I will talk a lot about opportunities because planning for taxes is just that—an opportunity to save. However, opportunities require action, so you must commit to learning and applying the concepts I'll discuss here to your life.

To make the most of this book, I have three key recommendations:

- **Learn to document your spending, savings, and strategies appropriately.** Cross your t's and dot your i's to set yourself up for success.

- **Don't get greedy.** Never slip into a legal gray area with tax-saving strategies that could make the IRS suspicious or get you into trouble.

- **Stay up-to-date.** Tax law is constantly changing, and we'll share any changes that impact the contents of this book. **Find the most recent book updates here**: http://updates.taxsavingsbook.com/

Now that we've covered that, we're ready to get started. Welcome to this journey of tax savings! I can't wait to share what I've learned over many years of helping business owners like you spend less and save more. More than that, I can't wait for *you* to see how much money you'll save with tax planning. After you have, you'll never think about taxes the same way again.

Mike Jesowhek, CPA
Host of the Small Business Tax Savings Podcast
Founder of TaxElm

▶▶ ACTION ITEMS ◀◀

Take Action: At the end of each chapter, you will find a section that looks like this. In that section, you will find action items that encourage you to take what you've learned in that chapter and put it into practice in your business. Use this as your reminder to make it a priority to take what you learn in this book and turn it into tax savings.

CHAPTER 1

TAX PLANNING VS. TAX PAYING

To talk about tax planning, we must first talk about what it is—and what it isn't.

The concept of tax planning versus tax paying is simple, but it's common to get it wrong.

The top mistake we at TaxElm see small business owners make is thinking they're already taking part in tax planning by filing their taxes. Often, this couldn't be further from the truth. *Paying* your taxes is simply compliance; *planning* for taxes is a strategy.

Let's talk about why.

Tax Paying

Tax paying is paying the government whatever you owe in taxes when you file your return.

Your year-end tax return reconciles what you have earned and paid (through withholdings and estimated taxes), and you report this information to government agencies. You do this at the end of the year for the previous year, then rinse and repeat.

Tax Planning

Tax planning is learning and applying tax-saving strategies to your business and personal life throughout the year. It's ongoing and evolving. You're thinking about tax planning not just when filing your taxes but when spending for your business, paying your employees and contractors, and even paying yourself.

You can change up your strategies if you find opportunities to save more money or your business grows and you need to recalibrate. Tax planning is all about finding ways to spend less, legally, on your taxes by better understanding the system.

Why the Difference Matters

If you just wait until the end of the year to pay your taxes and send whatever amount you owe without thinking twice, you're probably spending too much in taxes. Tax-paying without tax planning often leads to missed opportunities.

You need both. Paying taxes is essential, and you're legally required to do it. But tax planning is better for your business because it opens the door to more savings.

The tax law was written the way it was for a reason: to offer tax incentives to individuals to start and run businesses. Businesses help keep the economy growing and jobs available. Our job as business owners is to learn these advantages and utilize them whenever possible.

A lot of business owners neglect to apply tax strategies all year. They might even wait until the end of the year to look for credits and cuts. But if you toss out the tax planning mindset after filing, you're also tossing out a lot of money.

Tax planning needs to come first. Then, when it's time to pay taxes, you'll be glad you took the time to strategize. I've seen it time and time again.

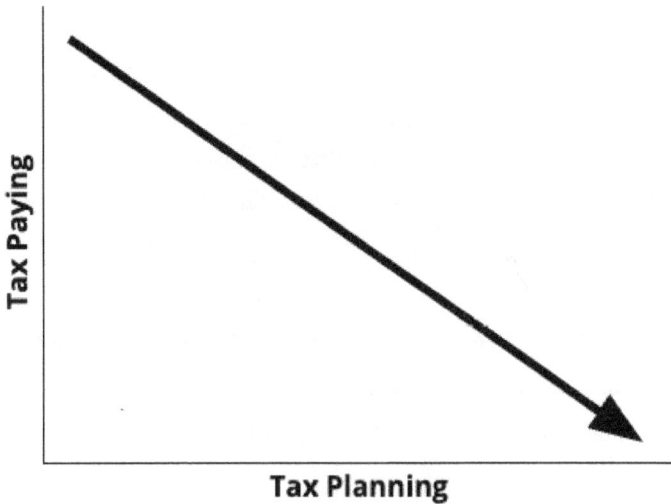

Tax Planning

Core Strategies and Advanced Strategies

There are two types of tax planning: core strategies and advanced strategies.

CORE STRATEGIES

Core strategies are essential tools every business owner should use. We'll cover these foundational strategies in depth throughout the book. These are:

- Easy to understand.
- Easy to implement.
- Free or inexpensive to implement.
- Available to business owners of all sizes.

Essentially, core strategies are the ones that businesses, no matter what size, should be learning, researching, and implementing to pay the least amount in taxes legally possible.

ADVANCED STRATEGIES

Advanced strategies come after core strategies. Once you hit a certain point in household income *and* have fully implemented all available core strategies, you can start exploring what we at TaxElm call advanced tax strategies. These:

- Provide significant tax savings, sometimes reducing a high tax bill to zero.
- Can be more complex and difficult to understand.
- Are harder to implement.
- Have some costs or investments associated with them.
- Tend to be riskier to set up and manage.

GENERAL QUALIFICATION THRESHOLD

To qualify for advanced strategies, you need to meet one of the following parameters:

- You have a household income (business, personal, or both) of at least $400,000.
- You are selling a highly appreciated asset with a gain of at least $750,000.

These strategies will be reserved for higher earners because the learning curve, associated costs, and investments outweigh the tax savings below this threshold.

Who Can Tax Plan?

All businesses—and I do mean all—can use tax planning strategies.

Tax strategies are available whether you're making $5,000 a year or $5 million. Some accountants make it seem like tax planning is only for the rich or too complicated to be worth it for smaller businesses. But that's not the case.

If you've ever believed that tax planning is out of reach, I want to challenge you to change your mindset. Here are some truths to keep coming back to throughout this journey:

- Tax planning is available to you (no matter the size of your business).
- Tax planning is worth it.
- Tax planning is just as important as tax paying.

With each chapter you read, I hope you find some tax-saving strategies you're excited to try and can start implementing changes immediately. If you do your best to engage with what you're learning and commit to finding opportunities, it'll be one of the best things you can do for your business.

Someday, when you hear the word "tax," you'll think about tax planning first!

▶▶ ACTION ITEMS ◀◀

○ **Know the Difference:** Tax planning happens year-round; tax filing is a once-a-year task.

○ **Start with Core Strategies:** Begin with easy, accessible strategies, and build up as your business grows.

○ **Set Your Own Pace:** Start small—implement one or two strategies at a time. Don't feel pressured to do it all at once.

CHAPTER 2

STARTING A BUSINESS – CHOOSING AN ENTITY TYPE

So, you've decided to start a business. Your head is probably swimming with ideas about what you will offer, how to push the envelope, and why you're doing this. But, while you're dreaming big, make sure you're also thinking small. Details matter.

With that in mind, here are some key things to consider when setting up your business that will impact your taxes and financials down the road. We'll cover entity types and pass-through entities, talk about how to report business income for different structures, and more.

Already started a company? Don't skip over this chapter. You might pick up something new or move on knowing you made the right choices.

But First—Where Are You Starting?

To understand where you're going, you must know where you're starting.

Every business has a different story, but many beginning stages look similar. Which phase you find yourself in now will determine how you can start tax planning today.

In general, there are two pivotal stages: a brainstorming phase and an action phase.

- **Brainstorming:** I want to create a new golf tool to revolutionize the sport and make me a multi-millionaire.

- **Action:** I created a prototype for a new golf ball with technology to track ball speed, location, and other details. I will start by selling it to golfers at the local course and, if successful, look for investors.

The person in the brainstorming example has a lot of work to do before creating a small business. They have a vague idea of what they're working toward but no prototype or plan for how to get there. *Every* business starts here. If you're in this stage, keep thinking about your big idea.

The entrepreneur in the action example is much closer to starting a business. They've begun researching and have an achievable goal and a plan for making it happen. If this sounds more like you, you're probably ready to start thinking about entity types, start-up costs, organizational costs, and bookkeeping. Start tracking what you're spending *now*.

Decide How To Organize Your Business

When you're ready to take action, one of your *first steps* should be deciding how to organize your business.

Choosing an entity type and structure is one of your most important decisions, so you want to get it right. This choice affects your taxes because it determines which tax advantages you're eligible for and how to file your return.

What Is a Business Entity?

A business entity is a legal organization established to conduct business. Each type of business entity comes with its own set of tax implications and legal responsibilities. You set up an entity by filing the corresponding documents for your chosen type at the state level.

There are many different types of entities, but most small businesses fall into one of these:

- Sole proprietorships or partnerships.
- Limited liability companies (LLCs).
- C-corporations.

You'll notice you don't see S-corporations on this list. That's because S-corps aren't entities. Instead, they represent a tax election for an LLC or a corporation. You, the business owner, can elect to have your LLC or corporation (entity) taxed as an S-corp (election). S-corps are unique and nuanced, so we'll spend a chapter discussing taxes and setup for these later in the book.

But back to entities. Each entity type has advantages and disadvantages and is taxed differently. Which one is right for you?

Which Business Entity Should You Choose?

There are many things to consider when choosing your entity type, including tax and legal implications. You should have this conversation with an attorney and do your research here. But to get you started, let's go through a quick rundown of each:

SOLE PROPRIETORSHIP

A sole proprietorship, often referred to as a sole prop, is a type of business that isn't officially registered with the state, meaning it's not a separate legal entity from its owner.

This entity would be the default status for any business that does not have an LLC or corporation setup. The most significant legal risk in this business structure is distinguishing between your personal and business assets. If your business faces a lawsuit from a customer, your business assets are at risk, and your assets, such as your home or car, could also be seized to settle the claim.

Advantages

- No paperwork to start the business.
- No annual filings with the state.
- Easier tax filing.

Disadvantages

- No liability protection for you.
- It is harder to get outside financing or business credit.
- Unable to claim certain tax advantages.

LIMITED LIABILITY COMPANY (LLC)

An LLC is a registration made at the state level. An LLC can be a single-member LLC (SMLLC) or a multi-member LLC (partnership).

Establishing your business as an LLC creates a clear legal boundary between you and your business, providing liability protection. In a lawsuit against the business, only the assets belonging to the business, not your assets, can generally be targeted to settle any claims.

At TaxElm, we see most small businesses set up as LLCs due to the defensive and financial benefits. Simply creating an LLC will not provide tax savings over a sole proprietorship, but it will lend legal protection and open the door for an S-corporation if and when the time for this makes sense, an option not available for sole proprietorships.

C-CORPORATION

A C-corporation is a business structure that exists as a separate legal entity from its owners, offering its shareholders protection from personal liability. However, it's subject to what's known as double taxation—first, the corporation pays taxes on its profits, and then shareholders pay taxes again on any dividends they receive. This structure is less common among small businesses due to this tax implication.

The primary benefit that attracts business owners to a C-corporation is the entity's potential for raising capital through the sale of shares, which can be particularly beneficial for businesses with plans to go public or attract venture capital.

PROS AND CONS OF INCORPORATING

Pros

- Liability protection for you from business debts.
- Easier to get outside financing.
- Tax election options (like an S-corporation).

Cons

- Additional paperwork to get started.
- Annual state filing.

- May be subject to local business taxes.
- More complicated tax returns.

Wait until you know you will launch a business to choose an entity type. If your business is still an idea, you don't need to do this.

But when you are ready, start with this overview of entity types and get your attorney involved.

TIP FROM MIKE

Quick Note: For most small businesses at TaxElm, we typically recommend LLCs. This entity type creates a solid legal foundation while opening the door for an S-corp election. Some professionals who typically choose LLCs include:

- Doctors.
- Lawyers.
- Accountants.
- Consultants.
- Contractors.
- Restaurants.
- Service providers.
- Rideshare drivers.

With any entity structure, we highly recommend working with an attorney to ensure everything is set up correctly and the proper documents are on file. An attorney will also help you understand operational rules to protect you legally.

How You and/or Your Business Will Be Taxed

One of the number one questions new business owners ask is: *"How will I pay taxes on my business income?"*

That is a fantastic question, and your entity type determines the answer. Depending on the organization of your business, you might pass your profits through your business to your return, report your business activity on a Schedule C form, or file a separate business return.

PASS-THROUGH

Most small businesses qualify as pass-through businesses or pass-through entities, meaning the company itself does not pay taxes. If you have a pass-through entity, profits from your business flow through to your return as the business owner, and you pay taxes on those profits as income.

Schedule C

Business Return

Form 1065
or
Form 1120S

K-1

Personal Return

Form 1040

Pass-through businesses include sole proprietorships, partnerships, single- or multi-member LLCs, and S-corporations. We'll talk about what type of business tax return (Schedule C, Form 1065, or Form 1120S) you'll have to file in this case next.

Note: A C-corporation isn't a pass-through entity because this type of company pays taxes on business profits at the corporate level, and its owners also pay personal taxes on dividends received. This system is referred to as "double taxation."

SCHEDULE C

If you operate as a sole proprietorship or single-member LLC, you'd report business activity on Schedule C as part of your personal tax return (Form 1040). A Schedule C is simply a supplemental form, which you'd also use if you were self-employed.

SEPARATE RETURN AND K-1

If you're operating as a partnership, multi-member LLC, or S-corporation, you'd first report your business's activity on a separate tax return. Then, you'd get a Schedule K-1 form that you would use to pass that activity to your return. This method allows all business partners to separate and report their earnings, losses, and other items.

Partnerships and multi-member LLCs file Form 1065, and S-corporations file Form 1120S.

How Pass-Through Businesses Are Taxed

We always see business owners with profitable companies keeping money in their businesses to prepare for growth. Then, when it comes tax time, they get hit with a bill and wonder how they could owe money when they didn't take anything out. How?

Nine times out of 10, this is because of pass-through entities. Remember that sole proprietorships and LLCs are both considered pass-through entities. **Pass-through entities are taxed on business profit *regardless of how much money they leave in or take out of the business.*** This is because you're paying taxes on the business's profit, which often surpasses owner draws.

To paint a clearer picture of what this can look like, here's an example:

EXAMPLE OF PASS-THROUGH TAXES

Let's start with some numbers for a pass-through business:

- **Business revenue:** $150,000
- **Business expenses:** $50,000
- **Owner draws or distributions:** $65,000

In this example, the business's profit is $100,000 (Business Revenue less Business Expenses). Therefore, the owner would pay taxes on $100,000.

In this instance, the owner only took out $65,000 from the business, but because the business's total profit was $100,000, they still must pay taxes on the total $100,000.

Let's now assume that in the second year, the business earned no income or expenses, but the owner drew the remaining $35,000. In that year, there would be *no profit*, so the owner would not pay any taxes even though they received the $35,000 because they technically paid taxes on that the year before.

This has been a simplified example of how pass-through taxes work.

How To Report Business Income

Where you report your business activity and which tax forms you use depends on your entity type, and so does what kind of taxes you pay—income taxes, self-employment taxes, or neither.

Here are some general guidelines for pass-through businesses, sole proprietorships and LLCs, partnerships and multi-member LLCs, S-corporations, and C-corporations.

PASS-THROUGH ENTITIES

When you actively participate in a pass-through business, you pay ordinary income taxes on your earnings. Some pass-through companies may also be subject to self-employment taxes. Self-employment taxes are the combined taxes for Social Security (12.4%) and Medicare (2.9%) that individuals who work for themselves must pay. Unlike traditional employees, who split these costs with their employers, self-employed individuals are responsible for the total amount.

SOLE PROPRIETORSHIPS OR SINGLE-MEMBER LLCS (NO S-CORP ELECTION)

In a sole proprietorship or single-member LLC (non-S-corp), you'll file your business information on a Schedule C on your tax return (Form 1040). You will pay ordinary income and self-employment taxes on the business profit on your return.

PARTNERSHIPS OR MULTI-MEMBER LLCS (NO S-CORP ELECTION)

You'll file your business information in a partnership or multi-member LLC on Form 1065.

Each partner will then receive a K-1 with their share of the activity, which they will use to report income on their tax returns

(Form 1040s). For example, if a business profited $100,000 in a year, and the owners split the partnership 40/60, one owner's K-1 would include $40,000 of the profits, and the other's would include $60,000. Whether a partner is a general partner (involved in the day-to-day business) or a limited partner (not active in the business) also affects how they are taxed.

- **General partner:** Pays ordinary income taxes and self-employment taxes on their share of the profit of the business and guaranteed payments.

- **Limited partner:** Pays only ordinary income taxes on their share of the profit but pays ordinary income and self-employment taxes on guaranteed payments.

S-CORPORATIONS

In an S-corp, you'll file your business information on Form 1120-S.

Each owner will receive a K-1 with their share of activity, which is used to report income on their personal tax returns (Form 1040). Every owner will pay ordinary income taxes on their profit share on their tax return.

C-CORPORATIONS (NOT PASS-THROUGH ENTITIES)

In a C-corp, you'll file your business information on Form 1120.

The corporation pays corporate taxes on the income of the business.

HOW BASIS PLAYS A ROLE IN TAXATION

The concept of "basis" in a pass-through entity can be complex, so I'll break it down to the brass tacks.

As a business owner in a pass-through entity, your basis is comprised of:

- The initial (and any additional) money you put into the business.
- Your portion of the business's income, which increases your basis.
- Your share of the business's losses, deductions, and distributions/payouts, which decreases your basis.

Understanding basis is important for tax reasons. It affects how you claim loss deductions, calculate gains or losses when you sell your business, and figure out the taxability of any payouts you get from the business. Accurately tracking your basis is crucial for correct tax reporting and planning.

If your basis hits zero and you receive cash from the business beyond this zero basis, you'll have to pay ordinary income tax. And, if you're actively involved in the business, you can only write off losses if your basis is more than zero. For instance, if you have a loss in year three but your basis is zero, that loss will carry forward until you have a positive basis (i.e. when the business makes a profit). When you sell the business, you can claim the complete carried-forward loss, including any losses previously disallowed due to a zero basis.

Now, an example with realistic figures:

Let's say you contribute $10,000 to start a new business. This initial investment becomes your basis in the business.

In the first year, the business earns a profit of $5,000. As the sole owner, all of this profit is yours, which increases your basis to $15,000 ($10,000 initial contribution + $5,000 profit).

In the second year, the business has a tough year and incurs a loss of $3,000. This loss decreases your basis to $12,000 ($15,000 - $3,000 loss).

Let's say the business distributes $4,000 to you as a cash distribution. This would reduce your basis further to $8,000 ($12,000 - $4,000 distribution).

So, at the end of the second year, your basis in the business stands at $8,000. If you were to sell your business at this point, this basis would be used to calculate any capital gains or losses on the sale.

Basis Calculation (Example)

	Year 1	Year 2
Starting Basis	-	$15,000
Contributions to Business (+)	$10,000	-
Business Income (+)	$5,000	-
Business Loss (-)	-	-$3,000
Owner Draw / Distributions (-)	-	-$4,000
Ending Basis	$15,000	$8,000

Remember, any further distributions you receive will be taxed as ordinary income if your basis hits zero. Also, if your basis is zero, you can only claim business losses once your basis is increased (by profits, for example).

Five Key Takeaways of Business Entity Taxes

That was a lot, but it boils down to five essential points. Here's what you should get out of this chapter:

- An S-corporation is not a physical entity type but rather a tax election at the federal level. You need either an LLC or a corporation to qualify to elect S-corp status.

- Most small businesses don't pay federal income taxes on the corporate level. Instead, they register as pass-through entities to allow the profits from their business to flow directly through to the company's owners before being taxed.

- Pass-through businesses can include sole proprietorships, LLCs, and S-corps.

- A C-corporation is not a pass-through entity, and it pays taxes on the corporate level.

- If you are active in a pass-through business, you will pay ordinary income taxes and possibly self-employment taxes as well on the profit of the business. You are taxed on the business's profit regardless of how much money you leave in or take out.

▶▶ ACTION ITEMS ◀◀

O **Identify Your Stage:** Determine if you're in the brainstorming or action phase to guide your setup.

O **Know Your Options:** If you're just getting started, understand the basics of sole proprietorships, LLCs, and C-corps to find the best fit for your business.

O **Analyze Your Setup:** If you already have an established business, review this information to ensure you're still using the most tax-efficient entity structure.

O **Get Professional Advice:** Consult an attorney to confirm your legal setup is correct and organized.

CHAPTER 3

STARTING A BUSINESS – SAVING AND PLANNING FOR TAXES

N ow that you know how your business will be taxed, you can start planning to pay your taxes. At this point, you'll ask yourself things like:

- How much money should I be putting away?
- What's the best way to save, and when should I start?
- How often should I expect to pay taxes?

These are the concepts we're going to cover in this chapter.

How Much To Save for Taxes

Unfortunately, there is no perfect amount of money to save for taxes that will work for 100% of small businesses. That said, there is a rough number I often give (because "it depends" alone isn't helpful).

How much to save for taxes: 35% of profit.

Why 35%? It is an average for a lot of small businesses. You might owe less, and you might owe more, but 35% should come close to what you end up paying most years.

The ideal thing to do is have your accountant run estimates so you know exactly how much money to put away. This way, you don't get stuck in the stressful situation of not having enough, and you're not tucking away cash you could put to better use elsewhere.

But you probably can't do that if you're just getting started. So, just keep this number in the back of your mind as a guideline (and bump it up if you earn a high income or are in a high-income tax state).

WHAT IS PROFIT?

If you're not sure how to tell what counts as profit, here are some basic rules:

- **Income:** This is money coming in from customers or clients. If you sell a service and get paid, it's income.
  - ° It is not considered income if you contribute money to the business for startup capital. That is simply an owner's contribution.
- **Expenses:** These are business-related expenses that help offset your income. If you're selling a product, it's the cost you pay for the raw materials. If you sell a service, it's your salary and other overhead expenses.
- **Profit:** This is your Income minus your Expenses, and it is what you get taxed on. You take all the incoming money from clients and customers, offset this with your business-related spending and expenses, and report whatever remains as profit to be taxed.

Important Note: Owner draws or distributions from your business are not business expenses and do not reduce profit.

Two Saving Mistakes to Avoid

It's never too soon to get ready for taxes, and it's always smart to make a savings plan.

There are two common mistakes I often see when it comes to saving for taxes:

Mistake #1: Not Saving at All

Many people who haven't owned a business before aren't used to saving for taxes. They've probably had taxes withdrawn from their paychecks (called withholdings), and the concept of paying business taxes is entirely new. They didn't put anything away and are blindsided when they get a bill.

Mistake #2: Not Saving Enough

Brand-new business owners also make the mistake of not saving *enough*. They made money and might have put some away, but it wasn't enough to cover their bill. Then they go to file their tax return, can't pay what they owe, and have to pull the money from elsewhere, scrambling to catch up for years.

Don't make these mistakes. Put away at least 35% of your profits (or whatever percentage your accountant recommends) from the start.

How Often Do You Need To Pay Taxes?

Many business owners don't realize until after their first year that they don't just pay business taxes at the end of the year.

The United States federal income tax is a "pay as you go" tax. That means you owe taxes as you earn income throughout the year. Think of a W-2. You earn gross wages, and then an employer takes taxes out and submits them to the government on your behalf throughout the year. Running a business is like that, except you're both the employee and the employer.

As a business owner, you're responsible for withholding appropriate taxes and making monthly payments. Even though you don't file your official return until year-end, you will have taxes due before then. These are estimated taxes.

ESTIMATED TAXES

When you run a business, you make estimated tax payments throughout the year toward the total amount you'll owe at the end of the year. Your year-end tax return then combines your business's activity to create a final number.

If you overpay in estimated taxes, you get a refund. If you underpay, you'll still owe money and may pay interest and penalties on the outstanding balance.

To calculate estimated taxes, you take your expected profit and personal situation to predict your tax bill. Most businesses pay estimated taxes at the end of each quarter.

Five Rules for Tax Planning

Now that you know some basics of how businesses are taxed, let's talk about five tax planning rules you should always follow to organize your savings and payments. Because the more on top of things you are, the easier *all* of this gets.

Rule #1: Start Bookkeeping Right Away

If you're spending any money on your business, track every expense to the cent. Learn about bookkeeping methods and tools, get professional help, and be consistent.

We'll tell you everything you need to know to get started with bookkeeping in this book.

Rule #2: Keep Separate Bank Accounts

Open a separate bank account (and credit card) specifically for your business. This tip is essential even for sole proprietors. Regardless of your business setup, you need to be able to divide your business and personal spending without any guessing. If you can't get a business credit card, open a personal card dedicated strictly to business expenses and treat payments as reimbursements.

And if you do any business spending before opening these accounts, keep a complete record of expenses coming from your personal account.

Rule #3: Avoid Commingling - No Exceptions

After separating your accounts, *keep it that way*. Don't let your business and personal expenses mix. If you get sloppy or make exceptions, you're asking for trouble, which will make things more confusing for you when filing your taxes. Commingling can also introduce mistakes.

But accidents do happen. If you accidentally use your business account for a personal expense, log it as an owner's draw or reimburse the business to keep records accurate. And if you ever accidentally put business expenses on your personal account, create a spreadsheet of them to record what you spend that you can use when doing year-end tax filings.

Rule #4: Keep Your Receipts

It's a little tedious, but it's worth it. Store physical receipts in a file in your office or take a picture of them and save them on your phone or in the cloud.

Receipts are *vital* in the event of a tax audit. They provide proof of activity and show why you qualify for deductions and credits you're claiming. To further protect yourself, write the following on every receipt: who, what, where, when, why, and how much you spent.

Not only does this help back up your business filing, but it also reminds you if you forget.

Rule #5: Ditch the Cash

Cash is hard to track and prove. Avoid using it whenever you can, which should be pretty easy to do in this day and age. If cash is your only payment option, get a receipt to document the business expense properly.

The best way to set your new business up for success is to plan and prepare for your taxes thoroughly. **There's no such thing as being overprepared!**

▶▶ ACTION ITEMS ◀◀

○ **Plan for Your Tax Bill:** Set aside a portion of your *profit* for taxes to avoid year-end surprises.

○ **Follow the 5 Rules of Tax Planning:** Keep your bookkeeping current, separate business and personal finances, avoid cash payments, keep receipts, and maintain thorough records.

CHAPTER 4

S-CORPS - DEFINITION, TAXES, AND BENEFITS

As promised, it's time to give S-corporations or S-corps the spotlight they deserve. Let's dig into what an S-corp is, how taxes work for these businesses, and reasons you might choose this tax status as a small business owner.

What Is an S-Corporation?

An S-corporation is a tax election, not an entity type. However, your business can only be an S-corp if you have established an entity structure such as an LLC or corporation (a sole proprietorship would not qualify for an S-corporation election).

The IRS also requires S-corp owners to take a "reasonable salary" for themselves. Essentially, you'd split the business income into payroll and distributions (or owner's draw). In the next chapter, we'll explain how payroll works for S-corps.

There are many other requirements besides this but remember these big ones.

If you elect to be taxed as an S-corp, your entity structure doesn't change. So, you could open an LLC and elect to be taxed as an S-corp, but you'd still be an LLC at the state level.

Why Would Someone Want an Entity To Be an S-corporation?

Great question! In our work at TaxElm, we often recommend S-corp status to small businesses aiming to reduce self-employment taxes.

To illustrate this, I'll explain how LLCs without S-corp status and sole proprietorships are typically taxed.

As a sole proprietorship or single-member LLC, you pay your regular income tax rate on the income of your business and self-employment taxes. For tax purposes, these two entity types are treated the same.

> **Regular income tax rate:** This is the normal rate you pay on all ordinary income, such as W-2 from an employer. Your rate might be between 10% and 37%.

> **Self-employment tax rate:** The self-employment tax rate is 15.3%, including Social Security and Medicare taxes charged on business income. The Social Security tax rate is 12.4% on the taxable maximum for the year, and Medicare tax is 2.9%.

Note: There are no deductions or credits to offset self-employment tax.

Sole Proprietorship or LLC (No S-Corp)
Business Profit

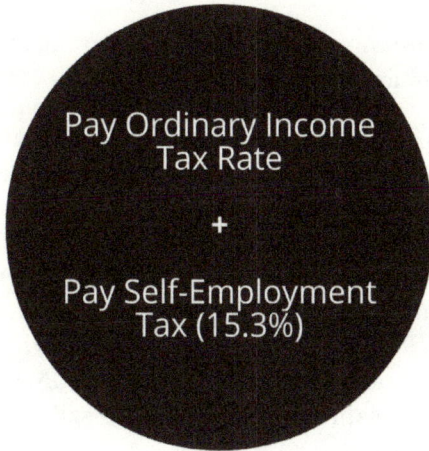

Pay Ordinary Income
Tax Rate

+

Pay Self-Employment
Tax (15.3%)

EXAMPLE OF SOLE PROPRIETOR OR SINGLE-MEMBER LLC TAXES

Let's look at an example of what a sole proprietor or single-member LLC might pay in taxes. We'll use a business profit of $80,000.

In this example, the business owner pays $11,304 in self-employment taxes plus their regular income tax rate.

This self-employment tax is one of the most significant disadvantages of a sole proprietor or single-member LLC setup. Soon, we'll discuss the benefits of electing S-corp status to save on these taxes.

How S-Corporations Are Taxed

There is no federal income tax for S-corporations at the corporate level. Instead, business owners pay taxes on the business's income on their personal tax returns. While they pay both regular income tax and self-employment taxes, they pay *far less* for self-employment.

Essentially, you split your business profits into two pieces as an S-corp: a (reasonable) salary and distribution. Then, you pay taxes on these separately.

> **Regular income tax rate:** The normal rate you pay on income, between 10% and 37%.

> **Payroll "self-employment tax" rate:** As an S-corp business owner, you're required by law to take payroll as an employee and will pay "self-employment taxes" on *this salary.* "Self-employment taxes" is not the actual term here; it refers to FICA (Federal Insurance Contributions Act) taxes, which represent Social Security and Medicare. You're paying both the employee and employer portion of FICA, which adds up to the same amount as actual self-employment taxes (15.3%).

Note: In the next chapter, we'll discuss what I mean by a "reasonable" salary in detail, but to sum up, S-corp business owners don't pay self-employment taxes on 100% of their business income—only the payroll portion. This is one of the leading tax advantages of the election.

S-Corporation
Business Profit

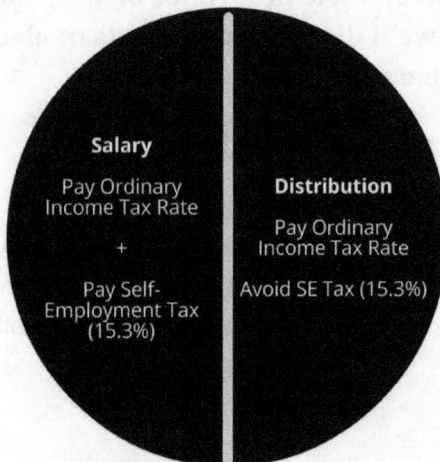

Salary

Pay Ordinary
Income Tax Rate

+

Pay Self-
Employment Tax
(15.3%)

Distribution

Pay Ordinary
Income Tax Rate

Avoid SE Tax (15.3%)

EXAMPLE OF S-CORP TAXES VS. SOLE PROPRIETOR/SINGLE-MEMBER LLC TAXES

Let's imagine the same business as before—with a profit of $80,000—this time with S-corp status, and imagine the business owner takes a reasonable salary of $36,000.

They're looking at paying self-employment taxes on the $36,000 payroll, which totals $5,508. The remaining $44,000 in business profit would not be subject to self-employment taxes, only regular income tax, leading to **tax savings of $5,376.** And you would see savings like this *every year*.

You may wonder: *If I took a salary of only $36,000, what happened to the other $44,000?* You would take that as a distribution (similar to an owner's draw), and it would not be subject to self-employment taxes. This is where the tax savings occur.

Of course, these savings are only for self-employment taxes, and you would still owe your regular income tax rate. But it's still significant.

Business Profit	$80,000	
	Sole Proprietor or LLC	**S-Corporation**
Potential Reasonable Owner Salary		$36,000
Payroll Taxes (FICA)		$2,754
Payroll Taxes (FUTA)		$420
Net Income	$80,000	$40,826
Your Portion of Payroll Taxes	$11,304	$2,754
Total Payroll Taxes	$11,304	$5,928
	Payroll Tax Savings	**$5,376**

In summary, by taking a reasonable salary and the rest as distributions, the owner reduces their self-employment tax obligation on income not subject to payroll taxes.

Should You Elect S-Corp Status?

Electing S-corp status probably sounds like a win-win at this point, right? So why doesn't everyone go with this option? In a few situations, electing to be taxed as an S-corp would not be beneficial. We'll cover those next.

WHEN S-CORP ELECTION DOESN'T MAKE SENSE

It might *not* make sense to elect S-corp status if any of the following are true:

You Have Foreign Owners

A non-resident alien cannot be an owner of an S-corp. So, if you have foreign investors, you can't elect S-corp status.

Your State or Local Laws Are Unfavorable for S-Corps

A few states and localities in the U.S. treat S-corps unfavorably, leading to decreased savings. And in these cases, you'd need to do a deeper analysis with a tax professional to determine if this election is right for you. New York City and Tennessee are some examples of places with such laws.

You Have Another High-Paying W-2 Job

The biggest reason to elect S-corp status is for self-employment tax savings. If you have a high-paying W-2 job, you may be maxing out Social Security taxes already, and thus, your savings would only be 2.9% (the Medicare portion). Again, this could minimize your savings under an S-corp unless your business earns more than $200,000. After $200,000, the savings often outweigh the costs of setting up and managing an S-corp.

You Expect Business To Decrease or You're Closing Soon
If you're expecting your business profits in the future to be low or you plan to close your business soon, the added costs of S-corp status won't be worth it.

You Plan To Go Public Soon or Have Many Investors
With an S-corp, you're limited to only one class of stock and 100 shareholders. An S-corp setup isn't likely a great fit if you plan to go public or bring on different investors.

WHEN S-CORP ELECTION DOES MAKE SENSE

Next, let's talk about times when S-corp status could be beneficial.

You Have Business Profits of $50,000 or More (and Expect To Maintain This)

In addition to your personal tax return, an S-corp requires you to file a separate S-corp business tax return on Form 1120-S. This return is more complicated than a Schedule C and thus costs more to prepare. If you don't have employees yet, you must set up a payroll system to withhold taxes properly, file payroll tax returns, and pay the respective taxes. The cost for this typically ranges from $50 to $120 per month.

If you are a small business making less than $50,000 a year, the added compliance costs of S-corp status will eat into all of your tax savings. $50,000 is a good profit benchmark for outweighing the added compliance costs associated with tax filing and payroll for S-corps. Having an ongoing expectation of this profit is also crucial. If you're making $50,000 this year but expect to make consistently less than that in years to come, S-corp status may benefit you now while hurting you later.

You Have No Other High-Paying W-2 Job

Most business owners' primary source of income is their S-corp—they don't have another job that pays them a high salary. This allows them to maximize their tax savings.

S-Corporation Summary

An S-corp is simply a tax election. It is not a separate entity. First, you must be an LLC or C-corporation, then elect to be taxed as an S-corp. Your company and entity won't change.

The number one reason to elect S-corp status is to minimize self-employment taxes. As a sole proprietor or single-member LLC, you pay self-employment taxes on 100% of your income. But with an S-corp, you take a reasonable salary and pay self-employment taxes only on this portion.

S-corp status might make sense if your business profit is roughly $50,000 or more. We set this threshold because there are some added costs to an S-corp (e.g., payroll and separate business tax returns) that can eat into your tax savings if you bring in less than this. At TaxElm, we would never recommend rushing into an S-corp if the added costs would wipe out the savings.

▶▶ ACTION ITEMS ◀◀

○ **Run the Numbers:** If your business isn't taxed as an S-corp yet, check if your profit is likely to reach $50,000 or more. Analyze whether an S-corp election could benefit you.

○ **Plan Ahead:** An S-corp is a tax election, not an entity type—you'll need an LLC or corporation first. If you're considering S-corp status in the future, set up an LLC or corporation now.

CHAPTER 5

S-CORP REASONABLE COMPENSATION AND PAYROLL

Interested in electing S-corp status for your small business? This chapter is about how to pay yourself a reasonable salary, a unique concept that's important to understand before making any decisions about your tax status.

Here's how to pay yourself in an S-corp and avoid common pitfalls.

Payroll Requirement for S-Corporations

The IRS requires S-corp owners actively involved in the business's day-to-day operations to take a "reasonable salary." This means you will be an actual W-2 employee of your business, otherwise known as a "shareholder-employee."

What Is a Reasonable Salary?

That is the $1,000 question. The IRS provides limited guidance on what qualifies as "reasonable."

Here's the description of a "reasonable salary" provided by the IRS:

S-corporations must pay reasonable compensation to a shareholder-employee in return for services the employee provides to the corporation before making non-wage distributions.

The key to establishing reasonable compensation is determining what the shareholder-employee did for the S-corporation by looking to the source of the S-corporation's gross receipts. The three primary sources are:

- Services of shareholder,
- Services of non-shareholder employees or,
- Capital and equipment.

Some factors in determining reasonable compensation:

- Training and experience.
- Duties and responsibilities.
- Time and effort devoted to the business.
- Dividend history.
- Payments to non-shareholder employees.
- Timing and manner of paying bonuses to key people.
- What comparable businesses pay for similar services.
- Compensation agreements.
- The use of a formula to determine compensation.

See what I mean? The IRS isn't clear about what it's looking for from S-corp salaries. But we've studied enough court cases and publications to have some reliable methods for determining a reasonable salary.

Strategies To Determine a Reasonable Salary

What does "reasonable" mean, and how can you decide how much to pay yourself? I often approach this with the question: What would you need to pay another person to do the job you are doing for your company? This can be a great starting point for a reasonable salary or replacement cost for your services.

TRY ONE OF THESE STRATEGIES TO BEGIN:

Option 1: Percentage of Income or Distributions

Use a percentage of net income prior to the owner's salary or distributions. This percentage should be at least 35% but can be 50% or more. Generally, the closer you are to 50%, the less risk of the IRS stepping in.

Example: If your business's net income before taking out your salary is $100,000, this method would give you a range of $35,000 to $50,000 for a reasonable salary.

It's important to note that this method is not a standard IRS guideline and could be challenged if it does not reflect the actual value of the services provided. At TaxElm, we like to say this method is a starting point.

Option 2: Market Average

- Determine the amount of hours you spend doing various business-related tasks every year. Examples include your job, administrative duties, and marketing duties.

- Find the rate at which someone doing these tasks in your city and state gets paid using data from the U.S. Bureau of Labor Statistics.

- Multiply that rate by the number of hours you work yearly.

- Adjust for special training, licenses, and certifications you have or are working toward.

- Add in other special considerations (e.g., other

43

highly compensated, non-owner employees).

- ° Example: If you are paying employees in your business an above-market salary, the IRS would expect the same for your reasonable salary.
- Crunch these numbers to find your reasonable salary.

Option 1 is easier to figure out. The biggest downfall is you don't have substantiation to back up your salary and explain why it's reasonable if you're audited. Option 2 takes more leg work but offers protection and substantiation in the event of an IRS audit.

Note: Both options can help you get started, but you should sit down with a tax professional to determine a salary that makes sense for you and your business. This is simply a starting point.

What Happens If Your Salary Is Too Low?

You don't want to pay yourself too little. This is why:

The IRS can reclassify payments made to shareholders from non-wage distributions (not subject to employment taxes) to wages (subject to employment taxes).

If the IRS audited you, you'd need to provide support to back up the salary you took as a business owner. The IRS would then determine if your salary was reasonable or too low. If it's too low, they would reclassify distributions into wages and require you to pay back taxes, interest, penalties, and fees.

If you took zero distributions in a specific year, there'd be nothing to reclassify. However, if you took a distribution the following year, the IRS would require you to pay the salary you should have taken in the prior year when you took no distributions.

Example

You took what you thought to be a reasonable salary of $50,000 and had distributions of $60,000. The IRS audits you, determines that $80,000 is reasonable, and reclassifies $30,000 of your distributions as wages. You will now have to pay FICA tax and any related penalties and interest on that additional $30,000.

How To Run Payroll for Yourself

You can't avoid paying yourself as an S-corp business owner and must ensure you're paying yourself enough. But how do you *pay yourself?*

At TaxElm, we always recommend using payroll software. This handles payroll tax payments and filings to save you significant time with payroll processing.

You have a few options for how often you take payroll compensation. You can set up regular payments or run an off-cycle pay run. These would be in addition to any distributions you receive as well. Here's what these can look like.

Regular Payments

The first option is to take regular payments on a weekly, bi-weekly, or monthly basis and run payroll to yourself automatically. This is like a paycheck.

Off-Cycle Pay Run

Take distributions as you need money and run an off-cycle pay run for your reasonable compensation at the end of each quarter. This technique moves a portion of distributions you took into wages, and you'd pay taxes on it.

Catch Up

If you made a late election, you'll need to get caught up on payroll for the part of the year you've missed. In that case, run an off-cycle pay run to pay yourself what you should have received so far in the year, and continue to pay yourself using regular or off-cycle payments going forward.

▶▶ ACTION ITEMS ◀◀

○ **New S-Corp Owner:** Go through the steps to determine your "reasonable salary" and run the necessary payroll.

○ **Current S-Corp Owner:** Reevaluate your "reasonable salary" with a fresh analysis each year to ensure it remains appropriate.

○ **Document for IRS Compliance:** Keep detailed records showing how you determined your salary to satisfy IRS guidelines on "reasonable compensation."

○ **Use Payroll Software:** Run payroll before year-end. Use payroll software to simplify tax payments, withholding, and reporting.

CHAPTER 6

S-CORP REQUIREMENTS AND DEDUCTIONS

I f you're considering moving forward with an S-corp, let's look at the IRS requirements to elect S-corp status. I've touched on some of these already in previous chapters.

Requirements for an S-Corporation

To be classified as an S-corporation, a business needs to meet these requirements:

- Your business must be organized as an LLC or corporation.

Note: Remember, S-corp status is a tax election, so you must have a company open first. If you're currently operating as a sole proprietor, you'll need to open an LLC or corporation in order to elect S-corp status and start claiming activity.

- Shareholders must be individuals, certain trusts, or estates. They **cannot** be partnerships, corporations, or non-resident aliens.

- All shareholders must consent to the election.
- The business cannot have more than 100 shareholders.
- The business can only have one class of stock.

These are a lot of requirements, but most small businesses qualify for S-corp status without issues. If you aren't sure, talk to an accountant about your eligibility and if it is right for you.

S-Corporation Deductions

S-corporations have a few items that must be done differently than other businesses. These include an owner health insurance deduction and an expense reimbursement policy.

OWNER HEALTH INSURANCE

As an S-corporation owner, you're eligible for a health insurance deduction if payments are set up correctly. You deduct the expense on the business side, include it in wages on payroll, and then deduct it on the personal side.

Let's break it down.

Step 1: Have the S-corp pay the insurance.
These payments should come directly out of the business bank account. You will deduct the expense as wages on the business side.

Step 2: Record the insurance payments as payroll. You will take that insurance expense paid and increase the payroll wages for the owner(s). If the plan ensures equal access and benefits for all employees (is non-discriminatory), no FICA tax needs to be withheld. This also helps you hit that reasonable salary amount. You will need to ensure your payroll provider knows you are recording insurance payments as payroll so they can include them in your W-2. This adjustment is typically made at year-end.

Step 3: Deduct the income on your tax return. Finally, you can deduct the income reported to you in wages for the insurance on your personal tax return (Form 1040, Schedule 1).

In short, you can deduct health insurance costs if your S-corp pays the premiums and you report this amount as income on your W-2. This allows you to claim the deduction on your personal return.

ACCOUNTABLE PLAN (A.K.A. EXPENSE REIMBURSEMENT POLICY)

You can also deduct any expenses you pay personally with an S-corp by setting up a system to reimburse yourself, called an expense reimbursement policy or accountable plan.

It's essential to reimburse yourself through an accountable plan. If you don't, that money may be considered taxable income. Here's how to treat different expenses:

- **Expenses that are 100% business related:** Run them through the business.

Note: If you mistakenly run a 100% business expense through your personal account, use the accountable plan to reimburse yourself.

- **Expenses that are not 100% business related (e.g., home office, automobile, travel, etc.):** Use an accountable plan to reimburse yourself for the business portion (Business Use Percentage x Expense Amount).

To implement an accountable plan, you just need to create a plan agreement and put it on file for your business. At TaxElm, we recommend using an accountable plan worksheet to help track items that fall into both categories.

▶▶ ACTION ITEMS ◀◀

○ **Confirm S-Corp Eligibility:** If you're planning to elect S-corp status, ensure your business qualifies.

○ **Treat S-Corp Owner Health Insurance Correctly:** Pay for it directly from the S-corp, add it to your owner payroll, and deduct it from your personal tax return.

○ **Set Up an Accountable Plan:** Put an official plan in place and follow the reimbursement policy to successfully reimburse yourself, tax-free, for business-related items you paid for personally.

CHAPTER 7

S-CORP SETUP AND RECAP

We've talked about pass-through entities. We've reviewed the differences between S-corps and other business types, including some reasons you might choose to elect S-corp status. We've also covered how to pay yourself enough to avoid issues and how to take business deductions.

First, I want to explain how to elect S-corp status, then take a moment to recap its benefits. At the end of this chapter, you should feel confident in your decision to elect or not elect this status.

How To Elect S-Corporation Status

To elect S-corporation status, you'll file Form 2553. Form 2553 is pretty straightforward—just remember to include all owners' signatures and information when filing.

You may need to file additional documents with your state to obtain S-corp tax treatment for state taxes. For example, New York and New Jersey require state election forms.

You'll want to file Form 2553 within the required time frame or request relief if you miss the deadline.

ON-TIME

To ensure your S-corp election is timely, submit Form 2553 within two months and fifteen days from your business start date or the beginning of the tax year you want the election to take effect.

LATE

If you don't file Form 2553 in time, you can request relief for a late election by:

- Writing "FILED PURSUANT TO REV. PROC. 2013-30" on top of Page 1 of Form 2553;
- Filling out Section I of Form 2553 for the reason of request; and
- Getting caught up on payroll for the time you missed.

The IRS usually accepts late relief requests if you follow these three steps.

Example: It is August, and you want S-corp status effective January 1. You can request relief for a late election and catch up on payroll since the start of the year.

S-Corp Recap

Pass-Through Entity: An S-corp is a pass-through entity. You pay taxes on the profit from the business on your personal return.

Annual Business Tax Return: You file S-corp activity on Tax Form 1120-S, which will include a K-1 to report activity on your personal return.

S-corp Advantages: You can save significantly on taxes with an S-corp by paying self-employment taxes only on your salary rather than 100% of your business income.

S-corp Disadvantages: You need to file a separate business tax return, you must pay yourself through payroll, and there are added costs for S-corps.

Electing S-Corp Status: To elect S-corp status, you must meet a few requirements related to your organization, shareholders, and stock before filing Form 2553.

Reasonable Salary (Payroll): S-corporation owners must take a reasonable salary as an employee (W-2 payroll). You have a few options for calculating this, and you want to ensure you are taking enough.

▶▶ ACTION ITEMS ◀◀

○ **Current S-Corp Owners:** Review the last few chapters to ensure everything is properly set up and organized.

○ **Non-S-Corp Owners:** Review the last few chapters to see if an S-corp makes sense for you. If so, take action to implement it correctly. If not, that's okay—just keep it on your radar as your business grows.

CHAPTER 8

HIRING EMPLOYEES

When starting a new business, many entrepreneurs try to do it all. They go solo for a while (sometimes until they can't) before hiring employees.

When you reach the point where help is essential, this chapter covers everything you need to know about hiring employees. Considerations will include choosing between contracted work and hiring employees, what factors to consider before hiring employees, and how to pay them.

Independent Contractors vs. Employees: Four Questions

Deciding between hiring contractors or employees is often confusing for new business owners. It's important to get this right and classify correctly on tax forms, but how do you know which option is best for your business?

The answer to this comes down to control. One person, the worker or the business owner, will ultimately have more control over the relationship and work dynamic.

Here are some basic questions to ask to figure this out:

- Who will determine the hours worked?
- Who will determine the pay of the worker?
- Who will be responsible for providing the worker with equipment/tools?
- Who will set the parameters for what work is done and how?

If you answered most of these with "me," then you probably want an employee. You will be in charge of how and what employees are paid, what they do, and how much they work.

If you answered most of these with "them," meaning the person doing the work, then you probably want a contractor. They will have more control over when and how the job gets done and have more say in how much they are paid.

Considering these questions, it's often pretty obvious whether you should hire an employee or contractor. Go with your gut, and you'll usually be correct.

DIFFERENCES IN PAY

For small business owners, the most significant differences between paying independent contractors and employees are payroll taxes and employment benefits.

Taxes:

- **Employees:** You'll withhold taxes from their earnings on the employee's behalf.
- **Independent Contractors:** The contractor is responsible for paying their own taxes.

Benefits:

- **Employees**: Typical employment benefits include paid time off, health insurance, disability insurance, and workers' compensation.

- **Independent Contractors:** No benefits are typically offered.

How To Onboard Independent Contractors

Independent contractors offer their services to individuals and companies on their terms. They define their work and pay and often work on many projects simultaneously. You may hire a contractor for a short-term project, a long-term project, or just as needed.

To onboard an independent contractor, you'll need:

- **W-9:** Be sure to grab a W-9 from a contractor *before* they start working. You'll use the information on this document to report how much you paid the individual to the IRS and, if applicable, provide your contractor with a 1099. Then, just pay them normally; no payroll tax withholdings are needed.

- **Independent Contractor Agreement:** Often, this is a written contract that defines the work to be done, the time frame for service, and other details of the work to ensure everybody is on the same page.

How To Hire Employees

Here are seven rules for hiring employees the right way:

- **Use payroll software.** Don't try to do payroll on

your own. Take advantage of software that makes things easy for you and automates most of the process.

- **Calculate and withhold payroll taxes.** This includes federal withholding, state withholding, Social Security taxes, and Medicare taxes. Typically, payroll software will calculate employer taxes for you.

- **Pay the employer portion of payroll taxes.** You'll be responsible for a portion of the taxes mentioned above. Again, payroll software will help you with this.

- **File reports and pay taxes regularly.** Make payments to the IRS and state agencies on time, monthly or semi-weekly.

- **File W-2s at year-end.** Do this early to avoid missing the January 31 deadline.

- **Get a workers' comp policy.** This offers benefits and protections for both you and the employee in the event of an accident.

- **Know your local and federal laws.** Every state has its own laws for hiring. Ensure you know the rules regarding minimum wages, termination, garnishment, and benefits.

S-Corp Note: Remember, if you go the S-corp route, you need to run payroll for yourself, even if you're the only employee. This is non-negotiable. Again, we recommend using software to simplify the process.

What To Consider When Hiring Employees

Even if you're sure you want to hire some employees to help your business thrive, there are considerations you need to make when planning this next move. Here are some tips for making sure you have the cash and preparation to hire employees and nail it.

HIRING EMPLOYEES CAN BE EXPENSIVE

When you decide to hire an employee for the first time, consider thinking beyond the salary or hourly rate you'll offer. There will also be hiring costs, taxes, and extra expenses on top of their paycheck.

Hiring

There are costs to recruit and find the right employees, and these can vary depending on how quickly you're hoping to hire and how many applications you have to consider. If you want the best of the best workers, you'll need to be willing to invest in finding them.

Taxes

You also have employer taxes to consider. We typically recommend planning for payroll to cost between 8% and 12% more than the gross earnings you offer. For example, if you bring on an employee and agree to pay them $50,000 per year, your actual salary cost will likely be $55,000 or more.

Benefits

You may also want to offer additional benefits like health insurance or retirement contributions you'll continue to pay for as long as your employee works for you. As a rule, the better your benefits, the more likely you are to attract and keep top talent. That said, additional benefits can cost you a significant amount of money. Be sure you know these costs upfront before offering them to your current or future employees.

Although there are several costs beyond salary to consider when deciding to hire employees, don't let that hold you back if they are necessary to grow your business. Weighing the costs and benefits is essential—use this information to make an informed decision.

PUT IN THE LEG WORK

Making an effort to find the right people to support you and set them up for success in the role is worth it. Here are three tips for doing your part as the employer when hiring:

- Learn to attract the right candidates—bad hires are costly.
- Take the time to create perfect job posts and know what you're looking for.
- Create "Standard Operating Procedures" ahead of time for smooth transitions.

SETUP IS THE HARDEST PART

If you ever feel overwhelmed when hiring your first employees, know it gets easier. Getting started is the most challenging part, but don't be intimidated—anyone can do it. To help simplify the process, we've broken it into a few steps:

- **Get your business ready.** Obtain an EIN if you do not already have one, register for an income tax withholding number with the state, and register for an unemployment account number with the state to get your business set up to onboard employees.
- **Obtain documents from employees and report your hires.** Gather information from all employees you plan to hire, including W-4s, I-9s, personal information, bank account information,

and anything else you'll need for payroll. You'll also need to report your new hires to your state using the state-specific process.

Once you've completed these steps and have everything set up in payroll software, paying your employees and keeping track of any associated expenses is easy.

HIRING OUT OF STATE IS FINE BUT COMPLEX

Good talent isn't always next door. Sometimes you have to hire outside your state. This is common, and we always recommend it for suitable candidates, but there are some special considerations to remember when hiring out of state.

If you find talent out of state, you will need to register for all the state numbers (e.g., state income tax withholding if applicable, state unemployment, etc.) in that new state. You may also need to file as a foreign entity in the additional state.

▶▶ ACTION ITEMS ◀◀

○ **Confirm Your Worker Classification:** Government agencies take this seriously, verify each worker you have is properly classified as either an independent contractor or employee.

○ **Prepare Your Business:** Prior to hiring your first employee, complete the necessary items, including obtaining an EIN, income tax withholding number, and state unemployment account.

○ **Budget for Employee Payroll Costs:** Account for additional payroll costs (FICA and unemployment taxes), which typically add 8–12% to gross earnings.

○ **Set Up Payroll Software:** Don't try to do it by hand; use relatively inexpensive payroll software to streamline the entire payroll process.

CHAPTER 9

ESTIMATED TAXES - WHAT THEY ARE AND HOW TO PAY THEM

E stimated taxes can be a confusing concept for new business owners—and they often trip up established owners as well.

But estimated taxes don't have to be confusing. Once you understand how they work, you can anticipate and plan for them so they don't sneak up on you or stress you out.

In this chapter, we'll talk about estimated taxes, including how to calculate and pay them to avoid surprise penalties and fees.

When Do You Owe Taxes on Your Earnings?

The U.S. tax system is a pay-as-you-go system. This means you owe money as you earn, and you'll need to make regular tax payments. As a W-2 employee, these are typically paid by your employer on your behalf (through tax withholdings on your paychecks).

For example, say you are a W-2 employee making $100,000 annually. As your employer calculates your paychecks, they are determining for you roughly what you owe in federal income tax, state income tax, Social Security, and Medicare. They then with-hold this amount from your paycheck and submit those payments to the IRS on your behalf.

However, as a business owner, it is *your* responsibility to make these payments each quarter and calculate them correctly.

Estimated taxes are a vehicle for paying taxes to federal and state agencies quarterly to cover the amount you earn or expect to earn throughout the year.

If you make $25,000 in the first quarter of the year, you owe taxes on this in Q1. You can't wait until the end of the year to file your return and pay what you owe. If you did this, you'd be late.

S-Corp Note: If you own an S-corp and take a salary for your-self, you'd probably pay taxes on your salary but not the amount you take as a distribution.

Year-End Tax Returns and Estimated Taxes

But what about your year-end tax return? How does that play into all of this?

Your year-end tax return puts together everything you earned and everything you paid and reports this to the government. Based on all this, you either get money back (a refund) or owe them additional taxes.

> **Refund:** A refund simply means you paid too much in taxes throughout the year. The government issues a refund to give your overpayment back to you.

> **Amount Owed:** An amount due after filing means you didn't pay enough taxes throughout the year and must cover the rest of your bill. This can also come with interest and penalties if your payments are overdue.

Think of your tax return as a reconciliation. You and the government settle up at the end of the year until you're even.

When Estimated Taxes Are Due

Estimated taxes are due on an *almost* quarterly basis. For whatever reason, the IRS doesn't recognize the typical quarters for estimated taxes. Hence, the "almost."

For estimated taxes, the quarters are divided as follows:

Quarter 1	Quarter 2	Quarter 3	Quarter 4
January thru March	April and May	June thru August	September thru December
Due April 15	Due June 15	Due September 15	Due January 15

Unfortunately, you won't get a reminder when estimated taxes are due. Keep these dates on your radar to ensure you don't miss them.

What Happens If You Don't Pay Estimated Taxes

If you don't pay estimated taxes throughout the year or don't pay enough, you may be subject to penalties, interest, or both. These fees can add up quickly, so make sure you are calculating your estimated taxes correctly and paying them promptly.

How To Calculate Estimated Taxes

There are two reliable options for calculating estimated taxes: the safe harbor method and the actual method. Both can work, but you might prefer one over the other based on your income and the level of effort involved.

SAFE HARBOR METHOD

The safe harbor option protects you from interest and penalties.

If you use one of the options below to calculate your quarterly estimated taxes, you can avoid owing fees at the end of the year even if you've underpaid.

There are two ways to take advantage of the safe harbor method:

- Pay **90%** of your tax liability for the **current year.**
- Pay **100% (or 110%*)** of your tax liability from the **previous year.**

    *If your previous year's adjusted gross income was over $75,000 (Single) or $150,000 (Married), then the safe harbor calculation uses 110% of your tax liability from the previous year.

    Here's how that looks in action:

Example: Sarah runs a small business and paid $20,000 in taxes last year. This year, she expects her income to increase, but to play it safe, she chooses the Safe Harbor Method to avoid any underpayment penalties.

- **Option 1: Pay 100% of Last Year's Tax**
    ° Since Sarah's tax bill last year was $20,000, she could simply pay that same amount this year to meet the Safe Harbor threshold, which breaks down into quarterly payments of $5,000. If Sarah's income last year was over $150,000, she'd need to pay 110% of her previous tax bill. That would mean a total of $22,000 or quarterly payments of $5,500.

- **Option 2: Pay 90% of This Year's Estimated Tax**
  - ° If Sarah expects her income—and thus her tax bill—to be higher this year, estimating her tax liability around $25,000, she could also meet the Safe Harbor rule by paying 90% of that estimate. This would total $22,500 or quarterly payments of $5,625.

By using either of these options, Sarah can rest easy knowing she'll avoid penalties, even if her actual tax bill turns out to be higher than expected.

Let's go through another, more extreme example. Imagine you earned $50,000 last year and paid $12,000 in taxes. This year, however, you win the lottery and receive $1 million (congratulations!). By using the Safe Harbor Method, you could still pay just $12,000 (100% of last year's taxes) in estimated payments and avoid any interest or penalties at year-end, even though you'd be significantly underpaying. You'd still owe additional taxes based on the $1 million, but you'd be free of any penalty or interest charges.

ACTUAL METHOD

The actual method for paying estimated taxes is more time-consuming but more accurate and avoids any surprise tax liabilities at year-end. It requires you to take your actual business income and other earnings each quarter and assemble a "mock" tax return to estimate your taxes.

Using this strategy, you use live data instead of basing your estimates on the prior year. This is why it's more precise and can be trickier and more time-consuming.

Many helpful estimated tax calculators are available online, but be sure to verify these results with a tax preparer.

How To Pay Estimated Taxes

This is the easy part. You can pay estimated taxes online through the IRS website or send in a check.

- **Online:** Set up an IRS Online account to make a payment. Sign in through a browser or use the IRS2Go mobile app to pay directly from your bank account or debit card.

- **Check:** Fill out Form 1040-ES and send it in the mail along with a check on or before the quarterly due dates.

Check your state's available safe harbor and payment options to ensure you're ready.

▶▶ ACTION ITEMS ◀◀

○ **Calculate Estimated Taxes:** Use last year's tax return or run current year numbers to estimate your quarterly payments.

○ **Complete the Payments:** Follow the quarterly schedule, and don't forget state income tax payments if applicable.

CHAPTER 10

PAYING YOURSELF

So, here's an important question you're probably already thinking about: *How do you pay yourself as a business owner?*

If you're entirely in the dark here, don't worry. A lot of successful entrepreneurs have been in your shoes. The good news is you have a lot of options for paying yourself as a business owner, and this chapter will break all of these down.

Options for Paying Yourself as a Business Owner

Taking money out of your business is simple. There are four different methods for doing it:

- Owner's draws or distributions.
- Payroll.
- Guaranteed payments.
- Dividends.

Each of these has different advantages and disadvantages depending on your entity type. We'll go over these types in detail, explain which entities best fit them, and cover some tax specifics.

Owner's Draws or Distributions

An owner's draw or distribution is simply transferring money from the business bank account to your personal account. This can be writing yourself a check, taking cash out, or something else. You're withdrawing business profits and moving them to use for yourself for non-business purchases.

ENTITY TYPES

For sole proprietors and single-member LLCs, these are known as owner's draws, while they're referred to as distributions for S-corporations and partnerships.

TAXES

Taxes on owner's draws and distributions can get tricky because these payments are not taxed immediately. You don't need to withhold taxes when transferring funds to yourself, so you get 100% of what you transfer. If you want to take out $50,000, you get the full $50,000.

However, this doesn't mean you avoid taxes. You'll still pay taxes on the business's total profit, including the $50,000 you paid yourself. And because draws and distributions are not expenses, these don't reduce your profit. So, while you technically don't need to do withholdings on draws, you will still pay taxes on them.

Here's a simplified example to help make this clear:

- **Starting Business Bank Balance:** $0
- **Annual Profit:** $85,0000
- **Owner's Distribution:** $50,000
- **Ending Business Bank Balance:** $35,000

In this example, you only had $35,000 left in your business bank account but still had an annual business profit of $85,000. The distribution is not a business expense and thus does not reduce the profit. So, when you file your personal income taxes at year-end, as a pass-through entity, you'll report $85,000 in profit, which you'll pay taxes on.

Payroll

Payroll is a business expense that a business pays its employees and, in some cases, its owners. As a business owner taking payroll, you'll be paid as if you were an employee of your company and receive a regular paycheck.

Always rely on payroll software to do the heavy lifting for you when paying yourself via payroll. There are many variables with payroll, including tax withholding, tax filing, and other payments to the government.

ENTITY TYPES

S-corp owners are *required* to take payroll, and C-corp owners often use this payment method too. A single-member LLC or partnership, not taxed as an S-corp, is not allowed, by law, to pay its owners via payroll.

TAXES

Because payroll is a business expense, it reduces a business's overall income. If you're taking payroll as a business owner, these payments turn into your personal W-2 income, and you report this on your tax return. Businesses must withhold taxes from payroll and pay these to the government on their employees' behalf.

When you onboard yourself as an employee, you will fill out a W-4. This W-4 tells the payroll software how much to withhold in taxes from your paycheck. Your payments will show a gross amount (your pre-tax earnings) and a net amount, which you receive after taxes are taken out (via withholdings) and paid.

Guaranteed Payments

Guaranteed payments, typically part of partnership agreements, are guaranteed to a specific partner regardless of whether the business makes or loses money. A business owner may take guaranteed payments as a form of regular earnings.

For businesses, guaranteed payments are tax deductible. The recipient will pay income and self-employment taxes on the funds they receive on their tax return.

ENTITY TYPES

Partnerships or multi-member LLCs may use guaranteed payments.

TAXES

Guaranteed payments work similarly to owner's draws or distributions in that they do not require tax withholding when transferred. Instead, the recipient is responsible for making tax payments at year-end or as quarterly estimated taxes.

Dividends

Dividends are less common for a typical small business owner and are also a little extra work. C-corporation owners may choose to take dividends in addition to or instead of payroll.

ENTITY TYPES

C-corporation owners usually take dividends in addition to payroll.

TAXES

Dividends are taxed at different rates depending on whether they are qualified or nonqualified. Qualified dividends are taxed as capital gains, and nonqualified dividends are taxed at regular income tax rates. Dividends usually come with some extra year-end paperwork (1099-DIV). Since most small business owners don't use dividends, I won't dig much further into this type of payment method in this book.

The image below summarizes the different payment options available to you depending on your business's entity type.

How To Pay Yourself	
Entity Type	**Payment Method(s)**
Sole Proprietorship or Single Member LLC	Owner Draw
Partnership	Distribution and/or Guaranteed Payments
S-Corporation	Distributions and W2 Payroll
C-Corporation	Dividends and W2 Payroll

Three Tips for Paying Yourself as a Business Owner

Hopefully, you're clear on your payment options and ready to begin receiving income. But before we move on to the next concept, I want to leave you with three tips for paying yourself.

TRANSFER MONEY TO YOUR PERSONAL ACCOUNT

If you need money for personal use, *transfer it* to your personal account and then spend it. Do not start paying for personal items from your business bank account. This caution goes back to what we've been saying about keeping business and personal expenses separate—it's for your own good.

DON'T BREAK THE LAW

If you operate as a sole proprietor, single-member LLC, or partnership, you can't legally pay yourself via payroll. On the flip side, S-corp business owners are *required* to take payroll. Keep the rules of your particular entity type straight, and you'll be fine.

DON'T OVERCOMPLICATE IT

Taking owner's draws is straightforward. Simply take money from your business bank account and put it in your account. Payroll is also a cinch when you have your software up and running.

▶▶ ACTION ITEMS ◀◀

○ **Determine Your Payment Method:** Decide whether you'll pay yourself through a salary, distributions, or a mix of both, depending on your business structure.

○ **Start Paying Yourself:** When the time is right, begin implementing your chosen payment method(s).

CHAPTER 11

BOOKKEEPING BASICS

Whenever I talk to a new business owner, it doesn't take me long to tell if they've started thinking about bookkeeping yet. And often, this is the last thing on a new business owner's mind.

But I'm here to tell you it should be one of the first. Bookkeeping is the backbone of doing business. It holds everything together from the moment you start bringing in money.

The good news is that getting started with bookkeeping is pretty easy, and you will be rewarded again and again down the road. Let's cover the basics.

What Is Bookkeeping?

Bookkeeping is keeping track of or recording every financial transaction within your business. You then use this information to create financial statements.

The two most common types of financial statements are income statements (or profit and loss) and balance sheets. Both of these are incredibly important.

WHY YOU NEED BOOKKEEPING

You need bookkeeping because you need those financial statements. Here are just a few of the *countless* things you use financial statements to do:

- Get funding from a bank.
- File your business tax return.
- Understand how your business is performing.
- See how your business spends money.
- Know who your top clients or accounts are.

The list goes on. Now, let's review the records you'll keep, starting with your income statement.

Income Statements (or Profit and Loss)

An income statement, also referred to as a profit and loss (P&L) statement, tracks income and expenses. It shows you how profitable (or not) your business is over some time. This is the basic equation:

Income - Expenses = Profit or Loss (A.K.A. Net Income)

- Income (or Revenue/Sales)
  - ° Money received from customers or clients for the goods or services your business provides.
- Expenses
  - ° Examples: Costs of goods sold, banking fees, contract labor, wages, consulting, travel, etc.

The best way to assemble an income statement is to track your income and expenses in a spreadsheet or cloud-based accounting software (my recommendation). You'll want to do this from the moment you "open your doors" to avoid missing anything.

INCOME STATEMENT EXAMPLE

Income Statement (Profit and Loss)
Your Company Name
Date Period

Account	
Income	
Sales	125,848
Total Income	**125,848**
Cost of Goods Sold	
Cost of Goods Sold	35,157
Total Cost of Goods Sold	**35,157**
Gross Profit	**90,691**
Operating Expenses	
Advertising	10,454
Automobile Expenses	3,264
Bank Service Charges	541
Consulting & Accounting	2,500
Dues & Subscriptions	1,479
Meal Expense	874
Janitorial Expenses	256
Office Expenses	735
Payroll Tax Expense	1,337
Postage & Delivery	125
Printing & Stationery	100
Rent	4,515
Repairs and Maintenance	1,133
Telephone & Internet	980
Travel	6,824
Utilities	576
Wages and Salaries	17,885
Total Operating Expenses	**53,578**
Operating Income	**37,113**
Net Income	**37,113**

Balance Sheets

A balance sheet tracks assets, liabilities, and equity. Essentially, it provides an overall summary of how much your business is worth. Balance sheets capture the financial condition of a company on any given day.

Assets = Liabilities + Owner's Equity

- Assets (What You Own)
  - ° Examples: Cash, checking or savings accounts, furniture, equipment, inventory, etc.
- Liabilities (What You Owe)
  - ° Examples: Credit cards or loans payable
- Equity (What's Left)
  - ° Examples: Owner's contributions, owner's draws, income or losses for the current year, etc.

Your balance sheet might not show much activity when your business is brand new, but keeping it up to date is critical even when there's not much to log. These, along with income statements, allow you to compile complete financial statements.

BALANCE SHEET EXAMPLE

Balance Sheet
Your Company Name
As of [Date]

Assets

Current Assets

    Cash and Cash Equivalents

Checking Account	91,705
Total Cash and Cash Equivalents	**91,705**
Accounts Receivable	23,504
Total Current Assets	**23,504**
Total Assets	**115,209**

Liabilities and Equity

Liabilities

    Current Liabilities

Accounts Payable	5,670
Sales Tax	466
Total Current Liabilities	**6,136**
Non-Current Liabilities	
Loan	32,670
Total Non-Current Liabilities	**32,670**
Total Liabilities	**38,806**
Equity	
Current Year Earnings	35,518
Owners Capital Account	5,629
Retained Earnings	35,256
Total Equity	**76,403**
Total Liabilities and Equity	**115,209**

Types of Transactions to Track

There are four main categories of transactions you'll track in bookkeeping. Some are required for bookkeeping, and others are just necessary to record for the purposes of running your business.

- **Bank and credit card transactions:** Every transaction that goes through your bank account or credit card (whether you spend or receive money) must be assigned to an account or category.

- **Non-cash or credit card transactions:** This could be an asset purchase or a loan your business took out for funding.
  - ° Example: You purchase a new Ford F-150 and take a loan out. You would record a new asset (vehicle) and the corresponding liability (loan) related to the purchase.

- **Invoices:** Although not required for bookkeeping, many businesses send invoices to clients to ensure they are paid.

- **Bills:** Although not required for bookkeeping, many businesses enter bills to track who they owe and when payments are due.

Depending on how a transaction is categorized—for example, whether it's a business expense or an asset sale—it might go on an income statement, balance sheet, or both.

TIPS FOR BOOKKEEPING

Bookkeeping is vital for every business. It ensures accurate tax filings, removes financial stress, and shows you opportunities to optimize your business operations.

In the next chapter, we'll talk about technology. Technology will play a significant role in your bookkeeping and payroll, and I'll share strategies for choosing the best software and apps.

▶▶ ACTION ITEMS ◀◀

○ **Set Up Bookkeeping:** Start strong with a reliable bookkeeping system to keep your records accurate and clear. Software can make this easy by reducing errors and helping you stay on top of things.

○ **Stay Consistent:** Make it a habit to update your books at least once a month.

○ **Leverage Financial Statements for Growth:** Your financial statements are full of insights—use them to make informed decisions and steer your business forward.

CHAPTER 12

CHOOSING APPS AND TECH FOR YOUR BUSINESSES

When we talk about apps, we're not talking about mozzarella sticks or nachos. We're talking about the technology or applications you can use to help lighten the load of running your business. Some people refer to this as a "technology stack."

I could talk about technology for hours without getting bored, but I won't do that to you. Instead, let's get into the basics of accounting and tax-related apps.

The Two Most Vital Accounting Apps

For those just getting started, you need two main types of software:

- Bookkeeping software.
- Payroll software.

If you're not doing an S-corp and don't plan to have employees, you can get away with just bookkeeping software and hold off on payroll software until you need it.

What Is Bookkeeping Software For?

Remember, bookkeeping is the backbone of your business. To support this backbone, you need robust software. The right tools make all the difference for clean, up-to-date, and accurate books and financials.

When it comes to bookkeeping, there are a couple of approaches you can take. You can keep it simple with a spreadsheet, which requires you to record income and expenses manually. This method works, but it takes time and leaves a fair amount of room for error and forgetfulness.

For this reason, I always recommend more sophisticated software for new business owners. These are typically inexpensive and make bookkeeping easier and less time-consuming. When growing a business, getting set up with good software is one of the best investments you can make.

Bookkeeping software helps you:

- **Import bank transactions.**
    - By connecting bookkeeping software directly to your bank (and credit cards), you can have all of your transactions downloaded automatically. Then, all you have to do is code or record them.
- **Create, record, and send invoices.**
    - When you need to request payment, most bookkeeping software allows you to create, send, and track invoices easily.
- **Create, record, and send bills.**
    - Software helps you keep track of who you owe and how much. You can upload

your outstanding bills and see who
you've already paid.

- **Create financial statements.**

  ° You can track and code all transactions
    with accounting software and then
    download financials for your business
    directly from the software. At the very
    least, you need these for tax time. But
    financial statements can also give you a
    pulse on the health of your business.

What Is Payroll Software For?

We've talked about the importance of payroll. There's no denying
how much of a difference a sound payroll system can make for
your day-to-day, and it starts with the right software.

Payroll software helps you:

- Onboard employees and gather hiring documents.
- Calculate and withhold employer/employee taxes.
- Pay employees.
- File federal and state tax reports and forms.
- Pay federal and state taxes.
- Send out year-end documents.

Other Accounting App Functions Business Owners Need

Bookkeeping and payroll software are the most important, but
these are far from the only apps you'll want to get to help you
run your business. Here's a list of some other tasks that apps
can handle.

- Bill paying.
- Accounts receivable.
- Receipt management.
- Mileage tracking.
- Expense reimbursement.
- Time tracking.
- Inventory/shipping.
- Point-of-sale (POS) system.
- Project management.
- Client communication.
- Internal team communication.
- Document management.
- Calendar booking.
- Screen sharing.
- Document signing.
- Password management.
- Marketing.
- Website design.

This list isn't comprehensive. The longer you run your business, the more types of technology you'll add to your toolkit as you get to know your own needs and learn about new resources.

When it comes to choosing apps, stay practical and choose technology solutions that meet your business needs without overloading your processes. Often, putting in the effort to find helpful technology is worth it tenfold. But don't go overboard and get "shiny object syndrome," either. Understand your software needs, research the best solution to fit them, set up your system correctly, and allow it to do the work for you.

▶▶ ACTION ITEMS ◀◀

○ Choose and Set Up Bookkeeping Software

○ Choose and Set Up Payroll Software (If Applicable)

CHAPTER 13

MAXIMIZING DEDUCTIONS

Maximizing deductions is one of the most important, if not *the* most important, tax-saving strategy there is. There are so many different types of deductions available to you as a business owner, including many you've probably never considered and even more you're not taking full advantage of.

In this chapter, we'll discuss many types of deductions you can qualify for, provide tips for maximizing your deductions and savings, and ensure you're clear about what's deductible—and what's not.

What It Really Means To Maximize Deductions

First, let's cover what it really means to maximize deductions. Because chances are, you've probably heard a myth or two about this.

A lot of business owners hear that they need to go out and buy things to save on taxes.

> *"Go buy a truck"* (you don't need)

> *"Go buy a new TV for the office"* (you don't need)

This is not true. **Saving on taxes is about maximizing deductions not by adding unnecessary expenses but by finding business purposes in your regular spending.**

Pulling this off comes down to the difference between after-tax and pre-tax dollars.

AFTER-TAX DOLLARS VS. PRE-TAX DOLLARS

We should always look for ways to convert after-tax spending into pre-tax spending. This approach provides substantial benefits for business owners, and it's a principle I consistently advocate. Here's what I mean:

After-Tax Dollars

After-tax dollars are money you spend after paying taxes on it.

For example, as a W-2 employee, taxes are taken out of your gross wages before they get to you. Then you get paid whatever's left, and your take-home pay is "after-tax" dollars.

If you then go and buy a desk and chair for your home office for this W-2 job, you're using after-tax dollars and getting no tax deduction for these expenses.

Pre-Tax Dollars

Pre-tax dollars are money you spend before being taxed. Pre-tax expenses offer upfront tax advantages.

For example, as a business owner, you have your sales or revenue—what you make—and your business expenses—what you spend. The business expenses offset the revenue and you're left with a taxed profit.

Spending on business expenses is considered "pre-tax" because the money has not yet been taxed. This fact is an incredible advantage for you as a business owner.

Let's go back to that example we discussed earlier, but now look at it from a business owner's perspective. Your home office contains many partially-deductible expenses, including utilities, internet, maintenance, and even lawn care. That desk and chair you bought are also deductible.

The Takeaway

Spending money on your business can save you money on your taxes because you're using pre-tax dollars that would otherwise be after-tax dollars. That is why you should always be on the lookout for business purposes in your everyday spending to qualify for more deductions.

Here's an important mantra we'll keep repeating: **The goal as a business owner is to turn as many after-tax dollars into pre-tax dollars as legally possible**.

Next, let's get into what kinds of expenses we're talking about when discussing deductions.

What You Can Deduct - Ordinary and Necessary Expenses

While running a small business, you will incur ordinary and necessary expenses you can deduct when filing your taxes.

But what does "ordinary and necessary" mean?

ORDINARY AND NECESSARY: EXPLAINED

"Ordinary" refers to expenses that are common and accepted in your industry, and "necessary" refers to expenses that are helpful and appropriate for your business (not necessarily indispensable). *An expense must be both ordinary and necessary for it to be deductible.*

An expense is ordinary and necessary if it's typical in your line of work and intended to help your business make money.

So, something might be deductible if it allows you to:

- Keep clients or find new ones,
- Acquire and retain talent,
- Maintain daily operations, or
- Otherwise keep your business afloat and growing.

Ordinary and necessary expenses can occur regularly or as needed. They do not need to be recurring to count.

Common Types of Deductions

The list of common deductions for business expenses is *long*.

Throughout this section, we'll outline various business expenses that may be relevant to your company and share planning opportunities for each.

ADVERTISING

Advertising costs support promoting and building awareness for your business. This includes various media types and promotional items designed to attract customers or clients. Most of these expenses are tax-deductible.

Examples

- Print ads (newspapers, magazines).
- Brochures and pamphlets (including design and distribution costs).
- Television and radio promotions.
- Media buys.
- Business cards.
- Google Ads, Facebook Ads, and other online advertising platforms.
- Digital media promotions, including website design and maintenance.
- Logo and brand development.
- Charitable sponsorship.
- Social media content creation and sponsorships.
- Podcast promotion.
- Vehicle decals and wraps for mobile advertising.
- Billboards.
- Email marketing.
- Influencer marketing.
- Event sponsorships.
- Swag (shirts, pens, water bottles, etc. with your logo).
- Trade show booths and conference displays.
- SEO and content marketing services.

Note: Political campaign contributions or lobbying expenses are *not* deductible.

PLANNING OPPORTUNITIES

Move Expenses from Charitable Contributions to Advertising

Typically, a deduction for charitable giving on your personal return is limited to a certain percentage of your income, but if you're planning to support charity, tying these donations to advertising might be an even better way to go. Often, this can lead to more tax savings than deducting donations. Try:

- **Sponsoring local events.** Put your logo on items or promotional materials that could lead to new business.

- **Hosting charity drives to bring in new clients/social media traffic/reviews**. Run a promo that says that you will donate a certain amount of money to charity for every new client, follower, or review.

- **Wear your brand.** Clothing is traditionally *not* deductible if it's appropriate for everyday use. But if you put your logo on your clothing for a corporate uniform, you can make it a deductible advertising expense.

COMMISSIONS AND FEES

Payments for services such as referrals, affiliate partnerships, and commission-based agreements are deductible if they directly relate to your business operations.

Examples

- Referral fees for sales or client acquisitions.
- Success fees for contracted business development.
- Commissions paid to external sales agents or firms.
- Affiliate or influencer marketing payments.

CONTRACT LABOR

Payments to independent contractors/subcontractors (non-employees) for services rendered are deductible. You will want to ensure you're tracking these expenses carefully, as there are many rules about how you pay contractors and stipulations about which write-offs you may qualify for.

See **Chapter 8: Hiring Employees** for more information about hiring contractors versus employees.

Examples

- Project-based freelancers (writers, designers, marketers).
- IT specialists for technology setup and troubleshooting.
- Professional consultants (business, HR, legal, etc.).
- Business coaches.
- Virtual assistants for administrative support.

Note: Employee wages would be separated and recorded under Wages and Salaries on your tax forms. For contractors, remember to collect a W-9 before you pay them and then send each one a 1099 at year-end.

DEPRECIATION

At a very basic level, depreciation is simply the process of spreading out the cost of an asset (e.g., vehicle, building, machine) over time as the asset's value decreases. When you buy personal property or real estate, you have a few options for deducting some of the costs. But not all purchases qualify.

As you might imagine, depreciation is not as straightforward as other deductions. This is why we'll dedicate a chapter (**Chapter 15**) to depreciation. For now, we'll keep it simple with a few examples.

Examples

- Commercial vehicles, trucks, or heavy machinery.
- Office equipment.
- Buildings.

- Large office furnishings (desks, chairs, etc.).
- Computers, laptops, and networking equipment.

- Technology.
- Industrial tools and specialized machinery.

Some things are partially depreciable. You *can't* claim depreciation on property held strictly for personal purposes, but you *can* take partial deductions. For example, if you use a car for both business and personal purposes, you can depreciate the business-use portion of the vehicle if you choose the actual expense method.

And some things are never depreciable. Land, for instance, is never depreciable, though buildings and specific land improvements may be. Purchases not expected to last more than one year are also not depreciable and would instead be expensed immediately.

EMPLOYEE BENEFIT PROGRAMS

Businesses can deduct contributions toward various employee benefit programs that support employee well-being and loyalty. This includes everything from plan design to implementation.

Examples

- Retirement plans like 401(k)s, SEP IRAs, and pension contributions.
- Health insurance (medical, dental, and vision).
- Wellness programs and health reimbursements.
- Education assistance for job-related courses or certifications.

EMPLOYEE ENTERTAINMENT

Entertainment expenses, provided they benefit employees broadly (not limited to executives), may be fully deductible. These expenses help build team morale and foster company culture.

In order to qualify, the entertainment must be primarily (50% or more) for the benefit of employees *other than* a tainted group. A tainted group could refer to highly compensated employees or an individual or family member of an individual owning 10% or more.

Examples

- Holiday parties or seasonal celebrations.
- Company retreats or outings.
- Recreational facilities on site for employees.

GIFTS

Some small employee gifts may be deducted. These are known as "de minimis benefits." These are tax-free for the recipients and can add up to savings for you. "De minimis" means small (around $70 or less) and not frequent.

Aside from employee gifts, you're also able to deduct up to $25 annually for business gifts given to current or potential customers. For gifts to a married couple, that deduction can double to $50 per couple.

Examples

- Gift cards to stores or restaurants.
- Gift baskets or small personal items.
- Wine.
- Flowers.

Note: Taxable items like cash, cash equivalents, gift cards, and coupons are not deductible when gifted to employees.

It's essential to separate payments made for employee gifts from those made to customers to avoid exceeding the different gift limits. There are also many unique ways to turn an employee gift into a valid, non-gift business expense (that can be over $70). For example, if you want to give iPads to your team, try pre-loading them with business apps, productivity tools, and company resources. This approach may allow you to deduct the iPads as an office expense instead of as gifts.

PLANNING OPPORTUNITIES

Use Your Branding and Logo

Try to find ways to put your logo or brand on items so you can deduct them as advertising expenses. Items that don't count as gifts include:

- Those that cost $4 or less that are widely distributed and feature your branding (think pens, desk sets, bags, accessories, etc.).
- Signs, display racks, or other promotional material the recipient will use on their business premises.

INSURANCE

Insurance premiums related to safeguarding the business are deductible, covering a range of areas from liability to specific property risks.

Examples

Premiums for the following may be deductible:

- General liability coverage.
- Professional liability (e.g., malpractice insurance).
- Coverage against business interruption or theft.
- Health and workers' compensation insurance.

Note: Life insurance covering your officers and employees is generally deductible **if** you aren't directly or indirectly a beneficiary under the contract.

INTEREST

When you take out loans strictly for business purposes such as investing, routine operational expenses, or other business needs, it is generally deductible. Interest is often reported on Form 1098, but even if no Form 1098 is issued, you can still deduct interest related to business debts. However, remember that interest on personal loans is not deductible.

Examples

- Credit card interest or finance charges tied to business expenses.
- Mortgage interest for business property.
- Interest on business loans.
- Interest on business lines of credit.

LEGAL AND PROFESSIONAL SERVICES

Professional fees paid for legal, accounting, or consulting services directly related to the business are typically deductible.

Examples

- Legal fees for contracts, IP protection, and dispute resolution.
- Tax preparation, accounting, and financial advisory services.
- Architectural consultations and fees.
- Creative services.
- IT consulting or systems implementation fees.
- Event management.
- IT services.
- Strategic business planning consultations.

MEALS

Meal expenses associated with business meetings or travel can be deductible, with the requirement that they are separated from any entertainment costs. Entertainment expenses are not deductible, but the meals around entertainment can often be deducted.

Examples

- Meeting with clients, vendors, prospects, etc.
- Dining when traveling.
- Dining with staff.
- Meeting with prospective employees.
- Office meals and food.
- Company parties and presentations.

This is only scratching the surface of meal deductions and how to save on taxes when you wine and dine for your business. We'll cover this in more detail later on.

OFFICE EXPENSES

Office expenses cover consumable supplies needed for daily business activities.

Examples

- Basic office supplies like pens, paper, folders, envelopes, sticky notes, notepads, and printer ink.

- Small tech accessories, such as chargers, phone stands, or USB drives.

- General organizational items, such as file holders, desk organizers, and binders.

- Cleaning supplies to maintain a tidy and professional workspace.

- Cameras.

- Projectors.

PLANNING OPPORTUNITIES

Take Technology Write-Offs

Technology is an often overlooked area. When buying electronics, think about what you are buying and if it would be viable for a business deduction. Computers, tablets, phones, microphones, cameras, and more can all be deductible if used for business purposes.

Deduct Subscriptions or Memberships

Find a business purpose for subscriptions so you can run them through the business. Things like Costco memberships, Amazon Prime, and journal memberships may all be considered office expenses.

RENT OR LEASE

Business rent or lease payments are fully deductible, covering any physical space or equipment that directly supports business functions.

Examples

- Lease payments for commercial office space or storefront.

- Storage rentals for inventory or supplies.

- Postage box.

- Leasing specialized machinery or tools.

- Safety deposit box.

Note: If you have a home office, there are different rules. Check out **Chapter 16: Home Office Deduction** for more information.

REPAIRS AND MAINTENANCE

Repair and maintenance expenses are deductible costs that keep a property functioning efficiently and in its original condition. Routine upkeep or occasional repairs both qualify. Maintenance preserves the asset's current state, while improvements, which increase value, typically need to be depreciated over time.

Examples

- Routine upkeep of office equipment.

- Supplies necessary for upkeep, such as cleaning materials or parts.

- Costs of service contractors for repairs or maintenance.

- Landscaping or janitorial services.

- Minor repairs to physical premises.

It's essential to distinguish between repair expenses, which are deductible, and improvement expenses, which fall under capital expenditures and must be depreciated. Capital expenditures increase an asset's value, extend its useful life, or adapt it for a new purpose, whereas repair costs are intended purely for maintenance and upkeep.

START-UP EXPENSES

Instead of waiting until you officially open for business to plan for taxes, you can start taking deductible expenses just about as soon as you've gotten the idea to start a company. Costs related to starting a business generally fall under start-up expenses and are deductible.

Per the IRS, start-up costs are "amounts paid or incurred for creating an active trade or business and/or investigating the creation or acquisition of an active trade or business." To qualify, these also must be paid or incurred before your business opens. You are considered "in business" and no longer a start-up when your first sale occurs. Then, these expenses just fall under operating costs.

There are two categories of start-up costs: actual start-up costs and organization costs. Actual start-up costs are what we've outlined below.

Examples

- Travel costs.
- Meal expenses.
- Training costs.

- Market analysis.
- Office supplies.
- Patent applications.

- Advertising fees.
- Wages or contractor labor for consultants and employees.

Note: Interest, taxes, and research and development costs do not count as start-up expenses but can qualify for other deductions.

ORGANIZATIONAL COSTS

Organizational costs are a category of start-up expenses you incur when forming your company. This would be if you are setting up an actual entity and not just a sole proprietorship.

Think of things like state incorporation or registration fees, legal and accounting fees, the cost of temporary directors, and meeting expenses. These expenses can be deducted and/or amortized depending on the total.

PLANNING OPPORTUNITIES

Start Recording Immediately

You have to wait until your business opens to start realizing the tax benefits of start-up costs, but you can begin accruing and recording these expenses as soon as you start thinking about a business. Even if you start recording start-up costs one year and don't open your business for another two or three years, you can still deduct those costs as soon as your business goes live.

TAXES AND LICENSES

Licenses or taxes that can be directly attributed to your business are deductible. These are fairly self-explanatory, but certain tax expenses must be recorded a little differently under specific scenarios.

Examples

- Property tax on business-owned real estate.
- Business licensing fees (e.g., health permits).
- State or local gross income tax.
- Regulatory fees required for business operations.
- Federal highway use.
- Payroll.

TRAVEL

Travel expenses can be deducted if they are necessary for business, such as client visits, employee visits, training, or conferences. These can be the costs of getting to a place, staying there, and eating while away.

Examples

- Transportation (automobile, airplane, train, boat).
- Lodging (hotel, Airbnb, etc.).
- Rental car.
- Tolls.
- Parking.
- Bus, taxi, Uber, etc.
- Meals (50%).

Note: For each travel expense to be considered necessary for business, there are a number of requirements that must be met. But rather than go into exhaustive detail here about deducting travel, we'll cover this in **Chapter 17: Meals and Travel Expenses**.

UTILITIES

Utility expenses essential to operating the business are deductible, even if the property is rented. Many of these will be the same types of expenses you pay at home every month or quarter.

Examples

- Electric and gas bills for the office.
- Telephone.
- Water and waste management fees.
- High-speed internet connection.

Note: Be sure to split out partial expenses for personal use as needed. For example, if you have a phone that you use mostly for business but partially for personal use, exclude the personal portion from your deduction.

WAGES AND SALARIES

Compensation for employees is deductible as long as it meets the criteria for ordinary and necessary business expenses.

Examples

- Gross wages and salaries.
- Other compensation.
- Children on payroll.
- Spouse on payroll.

Note: The employer portion of payroll taxes is typically a separate expense account but is fully deductible. This includes Social Security, Medicare, Federal Unemployment (FUTA), State Unemployment (SUTA), etc.

ADDITIONAL "OTHER" EXPENSES

We could go on for days covering various categories of other business deductions, but here are just some that fall into the "other" category.

Examples

- Cost of goods sold.
- Materials.
- Bank service charges: monthly account fees, credit card annual fees, etc.
- Charitable contributions made for business purposes to qualified organizations.
- Education and training (continuing education to maintain licensing or improve skills, education and training for employees, etc.).

- Service charges for accepting credit cards (A.K.A. merchant fees).
- Transaction fees (e.g., wire and ACH transfers).
- Overdraft fees.
- Laundry and cleaning expenses for uniforms.
- Board meetings.
- Collection expenses or fees.
- Franchise fees.
- Freight or shipping costs.
- Dues to trade or professional organizations.
- Subscriptions to publications (e.g., newspapers and magazines).
- Loss due to theft.
- Moving expenses.
- Outside services.
- Pass-Through 199A Deduction.
- Research and development.
- Royalties.

How To Maximize Business Deductions and Write-Offs

Maximizing business deductions is all about turning after-tax dollars into pre-tax dollars. That means finding tax advantages in the everyday spending you do for your business.

A lot of your spending that has a business purpose is either partially or fully deductible, and this lets you save on taxes without adding unnecessary expenses to your business.

Our number one tip for claiming deductions: Always seek a business purpose in each transaction and review personal expenses for any overlooked deductions.

Three Tips for Protecting Yourself

The goal of tax planning is to spend the least amount in taxes *legally* possible every year.

Taking deductions only works when you're doing things correctly. The IRS can and will audit you if they feel you're taking disproportionate deductions or that your expenses don't qualify as ordinary and necessary. This is why it's so important to cross your t's and dot your i's to make yourself bulletproof against an audit with any tax strategy you use.

Here are our top three pieces of advice for protecting yourself from or during an audit while maximizing deductions.

TALK TO A PROFESSIONAL - THIS IS GENERAL ADVICE

You may not be allowed to take every deduction you want. Be sure to talk with your tax professional before carrying out any strategy to ensure it's valid in your line of work and you're deducting the right amount. A valid deduction for one business owner may not be valid for another.

DON'T GET GREEDY - DEDUCT WITHIN REASON

Always do a "sniff test" when taking deductions. What I mean by this is that you should be justifying your spending to yourself as if you're being asked to justify it to the IRS. If you were in front of an auditor, would your explanation for an expense make sense? Would they agree that it's ordinary and necessary? If you have any doubt, you probably shouldn't take that deduction.

Make sure your expenses are proportionate to your income and that they make sense for your industry. For example, if you have $5,000 in income, $50,000 in travel expenses would be hard to justify as ordinary and necessary.

The bottom line is not to be afraid to use the advantages available to you, but don't be unreasonable.

KEEP GREAT RECORDS AND RECEIPTS - IT'S ALWAYS WORTH IT

As a business owner, you should always keep documentation of your business spending. This covers your back and lets you justify deductions by providing proof of where your spending is going and why. Here's how to do it.

- **Document details—such as who, what, when, where, and why—directly on the receipt.** Record the business purpose of a transaction directly on the receipt for it. The more information you include, the better.

- **Take a picture of every receipt and store it digitally.** Rather than try to hold on to paper receipts for everything, set up a digital folder for easy tracking.

- **Log receipts immediately.** Don't wait until the end of a business trip to get organized. Upload pictures of your receipts right away.

Don't miss out on business deductions. Use the tips in this chapter to start implementing tax-saving strategies to pay the least amount of taxes legally possible this year and every year.

▶▶ ACTION ITEMS ◀◀

○ **Consistent Review:** Revisit this chapter a few times each year to find opportunities to shift after-tax spending into pre-tax spending.

○ **Review Personal Accounts**: Look through personal expenses to identify any that could be reclassified as business expenses, creating additional pre-tax deductions.

○ **Document Expenses Thoroughly:** Save receipts, invoices, and proof of payment for each business expense, noting the business purpose directly on receipts when possible.

CHAPTER 14

BOARD OF DIRECTORS OR ADVISORS

E very business, regardless of size, can benefit from creating a board and holding regular meetings. This advice is not just reserved for big companies. Even a solo business owner can *and should* have a board!

Surprising to most people, these meetings are often *required* for your business. But don't just think of them as items to check off your to-do list. There are ways to save money and get more out of them.

Board meeting deductions are unique, so we'll give them a few pages of their own. In this chapter, we'll focus on leveraging board meetings for tax savings. Here's how to use your board meeting expenses and time with your advisors wisely.

Board of Directors vs. Board of Advisors (A.K.A. Advisory Board)

Most businesses have either a board of directors or a board of advisors (also called an advisory board), depending on their entity type. Traditionally, sole proprietorships and LLCs have boards of advisors, while corporations have more formal boards of directors.

A board of advisors is a group of people appointed to provide advice, counsel, and support for your business. It's a small group you meet with on a regular basis (monthly, quarterly, or annually) to discuss your business and obtain guidance. The members of your advisory board could be family, friends, colleagues, or anyone else whose opinion and experience you value.

A board of directors, on the other hand, is a group chosen to represent shareholders for your company. Your shareholders will elect them to supervise your business and act in the investors' best interest.

Benefits of Boards

Incorporating a board of directors or advisors into your business provides a wide range of benefits, including:

Offering helpful insight

Building a business can be lonely and sometimes overwhelming. Bringing in outsiders for new perspectives on company status and direction can go a long way.

Often, business owners also choose family members for their boards. This involves your family in your business in a structured, formal way.

Fulfilling requirements

Depending on your entity structure and location, you may be required to hold an annual meeting.

Ensuring accountability

Knowing that you'll need to report to your board and provide updates can motivate you to get things done. The last thing you want is to go to your board meeting and tell them you've accomplished nothing since the last meeting.

Supporting planning and alignment

So many small business owners get stuck in the daily grind of their business and neglect to do big-picture, strategic planning. Having a board can give you opportunities to think about the future potential of your business and strategize how you are going to get there.

Providing stress relief

Board meetings can help to relieve stress by showing you how many people believe in your business and making you feel less alone.

As a new business owner, it's important to use every resource available to you and lean on people who can help. Use board meetings as an opportunity to move your business forward and save on taxes while you're at it (more on that in just a bit!).

HOW TO SET UP A BOARD

For the most part, implementing a board is quick and easy. But it's important to register and structure your board properly. Consult an attorney to determine the type of board best suited for your business and the required setup steps. This includes documentation, choosing members, and structuring your board's operation.

HOW TO DOCUMENT BOARD MEETINGS

When it comes to deductible board meeting expenses, you have to be thorough and accurate when recording your spending. As with any deduction, your spending must be considered ordinary and necessary to qualify. Documentation can help you prove this if needed.

Here are two key rules for documenting board meetings:

- **Keep a record of meetings to outline what was accomplished and discussed.** Include attendee names, meeting location, duration, agenda items, outcomes, and any other relevant details.

- **Keep receipts and store them digitally.** Save these for every meal, plane ticket, and hotel booking.

The more documentation you can provide, the better. It's always best to be prepared in the event of an audit.

How To Utilize Board Meetings for Tax Savings

Board meetings have one main purpose: allowing you to discuss the current and future state of your business with board members.

But when you hold these meetings, you might be surprised at how many opportunities there are for tax deductions. Expenses such as travel, meals, and accommodations associated with board meetings may qualify as tax deductions. You need to hold these meetings in order to run your business, so you might as well save money in the process.

HOME RENTAL STRATEGY

As a business owner, you can take advantage of renting out your home for employee retreats, board meetings, client events, and more. If your business would normally pay for a rental space, you could use your home as that rental space. Your business can deduct the rental expense, and you receive tax-free income.

The 14-day home rental rule, also known as the Augusta Rule, is a special rule found in section 280A(g) of the Internal Revenue

Code that allows people to temporarily use their personal residences as rentals. It isn't going to apply to every business owner, but we do see it applying often. This rule states that if you rent your home for 14 days or less in a single calendar year, you don't have to pay taxes on the rental income. That said, you also cannot write off the expenses related to that rental use (e.g., utilities, cleaning services, depreciation, etc.) on your personal return.

There are some additional rules associated with this strategy, including:

1. **Primary residence.** The property used must be your personal residence.

2. **Business structure.** This strategy is designed for businesses structured as separate legal entities. Sole proprietorships aren't eligible to rent from themselves.

3. **Legitimate business purpose.** Any event or meeting held at your home must have a clear business purpose, such as a company meeting, retreat, or other function directly related to the business.

4. **Fair market value rental rate.** To avoid scrutiny, you must charge your business a rental rate that reflects fair market value. Conduct research to find comparable rental rates for event spaces in your area, and document this to support your rate.

5. **Detailed documentation.** The IRS looks closely at transactions between related parties, so keeping comprehensive records is crucial. Document event details, such as date, purpose, attendees, and agenda. Include any research that supports your rental rate as fair market value.

With careful documentation, you're able to turn a necessary business expense into a tax-free income opportunity, making the most of a commonly overlooked tax strategy. This list is not comprehensive. If you think you might want to rent your home for a business event, research carefully to ensure you are properly executing this strategy.

▶▶ ACTION ITEMS ◀◀

○ **Set Up a Board:** Decide upon either a board of advisors or a board of directors, depending on your entity type, and properly implement your board.

○ **Hold Regular Meetings:** Determine a regular meeting cadence (monthly, quarterly, or annually) and get them scheduled. Remember to keep detailed records of the meetings and associated expenses.

○ **Implement the Home Rental Strategy:** Explore ways to utilize the 14-day home rental rule (Augusta Rule), whether it is hosting board meetings, retreats, or events. Ensure you have complete documentation to back it up.

CHAPTER 15

DEPRECIATION/CAPITALIZATION POLICY

Depreciation: a word that can make any business owner (and some accountants) cringe.

Depreciation may seem like a difficult topic to wrap your head around. But it's more straightforward than many business owners think, and understanding how to account for it correctly in your business can make a big impact on your tax savings. That's exactly what this chapter is all about. Let's dig into what depreciation is and when it makes sense to implement a capitalization policy.

What Is Depreciation?

At a very basic level, depreciation spreads out the cost of an asset over its useful life. When you buy certain items and types of property, you often have a few options for deducting the cost. For some property types, depreciation might be one option.

- **Depreciable:** Property you can depreciate includes machinery, equipment, buildings, vehicles, furniture, etc.

- **Partially depreciable:** You can't claim depreciation on personal property. If you use something, such as a car, for both business and personal purposes, you can depreciate only the business use portion.

- **Never depreciable:** Land is never depreciable, although buildings and certain land improvements may be. And for purchases not expected to last more than one year, you'd simply expense immediately rather than depreciate.

Regular Depreciation, Bonus Depreciation, and Section 179

In general, you have three options for deducting depreciable asset purchases: regular depreciation, bonus depreciation, and Section 179. You would choose one depending on the type of purchase and the cost of the expense.

REGULAR DEPRECIATION

Regular depreciation spans three to thirty-nine years, depending on the asset type. In the year of purchase, you must apply rules, called conventions, to determine the month in which your depreciation deduction begins. The earlier in the year, the larger your deduction for the first year. Then, the rest of the depreciation will be spread out in future years.

BONUS DEPRECIATION

Bonus depreciation allows you to deduct a certain percentage of the cost of an asset in the first year and the rest spread out over later years.

Bonus depreciation that exceeds your business income within a given year can be carried forward into future years to help offset business income (and, of course, the associated taxes).

SECTION 179 EXPENSING

Section 179 allows you to deduct the entire cost of personal property in one year up to a certain dollar amount. That dollar amount is based on, and limited by, your taxable income and does not allow you to realize a loss for the year with the addition of the Section 179 deduction.

If a purchase qualifies for all of the above options, you can choose the one that makes the most sense for your business. You might decide you'd rather spread the expense out over several years with regular depreciation or take a larger deduction in the first year with bonus depreciation or Section 179.

It's also worth noting that you can take both Section 179 and bonus depreciation, but Section 179 must be applied first, and any amount over the limit to Section 179 may then be taken in bonus depreciation.

DEPRECIATION EXAMPLE

Let's imagine you purchased a brand-new computer for $4,500 in January. Here's how you could depreciate it with either regular or bonus depreciation:

With **regular depreciation**, a computer is considered a five-year asset, so your $4,500 purchase would be spread out across five years.

With **bonus depreciation** or **Section 179**, you could deduct more upfront in the first year.

Depreciation Example

Purchased Item: Computer
Business Use: 100%
Purchase Price: $4,500

	Regular Depreciation (MACRS)	Section 179
Year 1 Depreciation	$900	$4,500
Year 2 Depreciation	$1,440	$0
Year 3 Depreciation	$864	$0
Year 4 Depreciation	$518	$0
Year 5 Depreciation	$518	$0
Year 6 Depreciation	$259	$0
TOTAL DEPRECIATION	**$4,500**	**$4,500**

Two Rules for Depreciating

There are two important rules to keep in mind when depreciating. The first has to do with what purchases count, and the second has to do with when depreciation starts.

RULE #1: THE ASSET MUST SERVE A BUSINESS PURPOSE

Only business purchases can be depreciated. Property you have only for personal use isn't deductible. If you are using a property for both business and personal use, only the business portion is depreciable.

If you purchase an asset with the intent of opening a new business, you won't be allowed to depreciate it until your business starts. You don't necessarily need to have revenue coming in or be profitable, but you need to be fully up and operating.

RULE #2: DEPRECIATION BEGINS WHEN YOU PLACE PROPERTY IN SERVICE

Depreciation begins as soon as a property is placed into service. Property you depreciate must be *available* for use in your active business, not just purchased.

For example, say you purchase a computer for your business on December 15, but you need to send it back in to get software loaded onto it before you can use it, and it comes back on January 10. This would be considered placed in service on January 10, not December 15.

The date of service is the day an asset is ready to use, regardless of when you purchased or started using it. That means if an asset is ready to use but not necessarily making you any money yet, it is still considered "in service" and depreciable. For instance, a rental property is considered to be in service when it's ready for occupancy and listed for rent—even if it isn't actually rented or earning income for months.

What Happens When You Sell a Depreciated Asset?

When you sell a depreciated asset, you may have either a capital loss or capital gain, depending on what you sell it for.

To calculate this, you first need to find out your basis in the property, which is the purchase price less any depreciation. Then, your gain or loss is your sale price minus your basis.

Here's a quick example:

- Purchased a computer for $4,500.
- Took $4,500 Section 179 in year one.
- Sold for $2,000 in year three.

In this example, your basis on the computer would be $0 ($4,500 Purchase Price - $4,500 Depreciation), so your gain would be $2,000 ($2,000 Sales Price - $0 Basis), which would be taxable. This type of scenario is often referred to as depreciation recapture.

In that example, if you had only depreciated $1,500, your basis would be $3,000 ($4,500 Purchase Price - $1,500 Deprecation), and you would have had a $1,000 loss ($3,000 Basis - $2,000 Sale Price).

Understanding how much to depreciate is a critical tax strategy.

What Is a Capitalization Policy?

Besides understanding when and how to depreciate, you need to also know when it makes sense to avoid depreciating in favor of expensing. I'm talking about a capitalization policy.

Setting up a capitalization policy allows you to *immediately expense items under $2,500* without having to even worry about depreciation. The IRS refers to this as a "safe harbor."

The $2,500 expense rule helps you because:

- **No recapture period.** Unlike Section 179 expensing, there is no recapture period, simplifying your tax situation.

- **Immediate full expense.** Instead of dealing with depreciation, you can fully expense the item in the first year, similar to how you would treat office supplies like pens and paper.

- **Simplified records.** This approach streamlines your tax and business records by eliminating the need to track these smaller assets over time. You won't have the assets cluttering your books.

Every business owner should take advantage of this safe harbor. Often, expensing smaller purchases makes more sense than depreciating them.

HOW TO USE SAFE HARBOR EXPENSING

To take advantage of this safe harbor, you need to have a capitalization policy in place, and you must make an election on your tax return.

Have a Capitalization Policy in Place

You need to put a written capitalization policy in place at the beginning of the year to determine which asset purchases will be expensed versus capitalized throughout the year. Here are three steps for doing this.

- **Indicate expensing up to the $2,500 IRS safe-harbor limit.** You can choose a lower number if you wish, but $2,500 is the maximum (and what most accountants would recommend).

- **Follow your policy for *all* asset purchases that meet the thresholds.** You cannot pick and choose some to depreciate and some to expense.

- **Keep invoices on file.** This is especially important if you have multiple purchases on one payment.

Make an Election on Your Tax Return

When you file your tax return, you will want to make an election to use safe harbor expensing. This is simply a statement you include with the filing to indicate your plans.

CAPITALIZATION POLICY EXAMPLE

Imagine you bought two new desks for $4,400 ($2,200 each). Without safe harbor, you would need to capitalize and depreciate each desk and keep them on your books as an asset.

With safe harbor, you would simply expense them immediately as "office expenses." Your life is easier. Remember, the invoice needs to prove it was two purchases at $2,200 and not one at $4,400, which would exceed the safe harbor amount.

FOUR KEY TAKEAWAYS OF DEPRECIATION

To sum up this chapter, here are four key takeaways:

- Depreciation cannot begin until you have an active business.

- Depreciation for business property begins once the property is placed in service (available for use in the business).

- If you use property for both business and personal purposes, you can depreciate only the business-use portion.

- Implement a capitalization policy in your business to take advantage of the IRS safe harbor rule so you can immediately expense asset purchases under $2,500 without having to worry about depreciation.

That's everything you need to know to get started with depreciation! Next up, we'll cover another area of deductions we get many questions about at TaxElm—working from home.

▶▶ ACTION ITEMS ◀◀

○ **Buying Assets?** Determine the optimal depreciation method for each asset purchase. Document the business purpose and confirm the asset is placed in service.

○ **Create a Capitalization Policy:** Draft a written policy to expense purchases up to $2,500, which supports compliance and simplifies record-keeping. Be sure to make the necessary election on your tax return to apply the safe harbor rule to eligible expenses.

CHAPTER 16

HOME OFFICE DEDUCTION

There is a lot of confusion among business owners about the home office deduction. Maybe this is because there is conflicting advice about the risks. Maybe it's because so many people now work from home (even if only a few days a week) and are uncertain about what truly counts as a home office.

Whatever the case, we'll use this chapter to clear up confusion and explain why the home office deduction is a perfectly safe and advantageous tax strategy—when executed properly.

What Qualifies as a Home Office?

There are two main requirements for a room in your home to qualify for the home office deduction.

- It must be used *exclusively for business and on a regular basis*.
- It must be the *principal place you do business*.

EXCLUSIVELY FOR BUSINESS AND ON A REGULAR BASIS

"Exclusively for business" means your home office is not for personal use. This is why you can't consider your living room a home office, even if it's where you set up a computer, if it's also where you watch TV and play with your kids.

You could, however, use a portion of a room as long as you can provide support to prove that the portion or section is only for business and never personal use.

"Regular basis" simply means you have to use the space often for business. If your business requires you to travel almost every day, and you only work from home once or twice a quarter, it can't qualify as a home office.

PRINCIPAL PLACE OF BUSINESS

If you meet with clients, customers, patients, or anyone else to conduct business in your home office, you easily pass this test.

This test used to be harder to meet if you had a separate physical office outside of your home. However, after some recent tax cases, it has become easier due to the idea of an "administrative or management" office.

The "principal place of business" requirement would qualify you for the deduction if you have a home office used for administrative or management duties and there is no other fixed location where *substantial* administrative or management activities are conducted.

Note: If you do administrative or management activities at another location, you would still qualify as long as the work is not substantial (or occurring a majority of the time) at the other location.

Let's say you're a veterinarian, and you see patients and do your charting at your clinic. But when you come home, you answer emails, complete bookkeeping, and wrap up a few other small tasks in your home office. All of this would fall under administrative activities.

This deduction is fairly easy to qualify for, and many business owners are eligible.

HOW TO HANDLE MULTIPLE OFFICES

If you have an office in your home and an office outside your home, but you still want to take this deduction, limit your administrative or managerial tasks to your home office. You can still do other work at another office.

How To Calculate the Home Office Deduction

Now that you know if you qualify, let's discuss how to calculate your home office deduction. There are two main ways to do this: the simplified method and the actual method.

Simplified Method

Deduct **$5 per square foot** of qualifying office space (up to a maximum of 300 square feet or $1,500 annually).

This method allows you to still claim all of your home's property taxes and mortgage interest on your personal return, should you qualify. And if you sell your house and use this method, you don't need to recapture depreciation.

Actual Method

This method requires you to use a couple of equations to capture your business use more precisely. Here are the steps.

- **Find your business use percentage (BUP) using this formula:**

  BUP = Home Office Square Footage / Total Home Square Footage

- **Multiply your BUP by all relevant and necessary expenses.** This can be mortgage interest, property taxes, rent, home insurance, utilities, HOA/condo dues, repairs, maintenance, depreciation, garbage pickup, security fees, lawn care, etc.

The actual method requires more detailed record keeping and may be subject to depreciation recapture down the road if depreciation was taken and you sell your home. But even then, it often yields a higher deduction than the simplified method.

EXAMPLE OF HOME OFFICE CALCULATION

See the following examples of both methods using a home office with the following specs:

- **Office Square Footage:** 250 square feet
- **Total Home Square Footage:** 2,000 square feet
- **Total Home Expenses:** $31,800 per year

Example Using Simplified Method
- 250 square feet x $5 per square foot = **$1,250 home office deduction**

Example Using Actual Method

- Business Use Percentage (BUP) = 12.5% (250/2,000)

- Expenses: $31,800

- 12.5% (BUP) x $31,800 (Costs): **$3,975 home office deduction**

As you can see, the actual method provides a much better home office deduction here. But that won't always be the case, so test out both calculations to decide which works best for you.

Where To Claim the Home Office Deduction

Now that you've crunched the numbers, let's go to the final step: claiming this deduction. How you do this depends on the entity structure of your business and which home office deduction calculation you used.

- **Sole proprietor or single-member LLC:** Use Form 8829 (actual method) or claim the deduction directly on Page 1 of Schedule C (simplified method).

- **S-Corporation:** Use an accountable plan (see **Chapter 6: S-Corp Requirements and Deductions** for details) to reimburse yourself as the owner for the use of the office. This will be an expense to the business and not taxable to you as long as you are utilizing an accountable plan.

Why You Should Take the Home Office Deduction

The home office deduction is *not* an audit risk if you are doing it right. It *is* a smart and easy way to save on taxes.

Claiming a home office deduction can also provide opportunities to take advantage of other deductions, such as automobile expenses and business miles. When you leave your home office for business purposes, that's now deductible business mileage because you have to leave your home office.

This deduction is definitely worth looking into and taking full advantage of. Keep a log of spending, take photos of your office, determine the best calculation method to use, and start saving more on taxes!

▶▶ ACTION ITEMS ◀◀

○ **Confirm Home Office Eligibility:** Ensure your workspace is used exclusively and regularly for business and serves as your principal place of business.

○ **Calculate and Take the Deduction:** Decide whether the simplified or actual expense method best fits your needs. Then, depending on your entity type, apply the home office deduction accurately on your tax return.

CHAPTER 17

MEALS AND TRAVEL EXPENSES

As a business owner, you probably spend a decent chunk of change meeting clients for drinks, taking employees out to eat, hosting parties and events, traveling to conferences, and the like. The fact of the matter is that meals and entertainment are not insignificant expenses for small business owners. And there are many opportunities to write these off.

This chapter is going to focus on maximizing deductions for meals, entertainment, and travel.

What Is a Meal Expense?

A meal expense includes food or beverages consumed for a legitimate business purpose. These expenses can be either partially or fully deductible, depending on which category they fall into.

Here are the five main categories of meal expenses and how much you can deduct for each:

- **Dining with a prospect, client, vendor, etc.:** 50% deductible
- **Dining when traveling:** 50% deductible

Note: It must be overnight travel and outside of your normal commute

- **Dining with staff:** 50% deductible
- **Office meals/food:** 50% deductible
- **Company parties/presentations (primarily for the benefit of employees):** 100% deductible

Meal Expense

	Zero	50%	100%
Dining with a Prospect		X	
Dining with a Client		X	
Dining with a Vendor		X	
Dining with Staff		X	
Dining when Traveling (Must be overnight and outside of normal commute)		X	
Office Meals & Food		X	
Company Party or Event (Primarily for Benefit of Employees)			X
Entertainment	X		
Baseball Game Tickets	X		
Food at Baseball Game with Client, Staff, Vendor		X	
Meals Served for Marketing Presentation			X

MEAL EXPENSE EXAMPLES

- Meeting with a current or potential client.
- Meeting with a current or potential employee.
- Employee team meals.

- Hosted meetings (Chamber, BNI, networking, etc.).
- Year-end parties.
- Food and drinks at golf outings.
- Team building recreational events.
- Meals at a country club with clients.
- Meals at an office cafeteria.
- Meals cooked in a hotel on business trips.

How To Maximize Deductions for Meal Expenses

Deducting meal expenses is all about strategizing where you go and who you take when you eat or drink on the business's dime. Here is some basic advice I give all TaxElm members for maximizing meal expense deductions: Talk business and choose group outings over solo outings.

Talk Business

From now on, everyone is a potential or current business client. Start talking business and asking for referrals over meals and beverages. Are you grabbing dinner with a client or potential client who also happens to be a friend or family member? Think differently about the purpose of every meal to make this work for your industry niche. Remember to always document the business purpose.

Turn Solo Meals and Drinks into Group Events

Going through a drive-through restaurant by yourself on your way to work isn't deductible. But if you're on a business trip, meeting with coworkers, or taking a client out, you can expense at least a portion of that meal (though I wouldn't recommend taking a real potential client through a drive-through unless it's *really* good!).

What Is a Travel Expense?

Expenses incurred by you or your employees while traveling for business purposes may qualify as deductible travel expenses.

For a trip to be considered business travel, an individual must be away from their "tax home" substantially longer than an ordinary day's work, and they must need to get sleep or rest to meet the demands of the workday while away. A "tax home" is the city or area in which an individual regularly works, regardless of where they live.

Travel costs can include:

- Transportation (rental car, airplane, train, boat, parking, rideshare, tolls).
- Lodging (hotel, Airbnb, etc.).
- Meals.

Travel reasons can include:

- Meeting with a vendor.
- Meeting with a client.
- Corporate or board meetings.
- Attending a conference or training.
- Visiting a rental you own or are considering owning.

RULES FOR BUSINESS TRAVEL

- **Business day:** For a day to be considered a "business day," most of the workday (four hours and one minute if you typically work eight-hour days) must be spent on business.

- **Overnight:** To be in "travel status," you must be away from your home and principal place of business overnight.

- **Travel days:** Days spent traveling to or from your destination are considered business days if the total number of days spent on business tasks during your trip exceeds the number of personal days. For international trips greater than seven days, more than 75% of the trip must be business-related.

- **Weekends and holidays:** If you have a weekend or holiday sandwiched between two business days, these are considered business days as well, even if spent personally.

How To Maximize Deductions for Travel Expenses

Travel expenses add up quickly, and many of them are unavoidable. But there are plenty of ways to save on taxes while traveling if you think strategically.

Spend Business Days on Personal Trips

You can deduct food and lodging on business days, even on personal trips, as long as you can prove that these expenses were business-related. For example, if you go on a family vacation to San Diego but spend an afternoon meeting with customers or prospective customers, your costs for that afternoon (meals, Uber, parking, etc.) could be deducted. The rest of your trip, including your travel to and from San Diego, would not be deductible if you spent more personal days than business days on the trip.

This is a good reason to do business on vacation when the opportunity presents itself.

Plan Out Your Trips

Whenever you have travel plans, plan ahead to make them qualify as business trips, and keep a diary of the business days. If you have family (not involved in the business) traveling with you, their costs are not deductible.

Finally, I want to close out this chapter with a bit of advice: Don't overdo it. It's easy to get greedy when deducting meal and travel expenses, but don't go overboard. As with any write-offs, you need to find the right balance between being aggressive and being conservative.

What About Entertainment Expenses?

As of 2018, entertainment expenses are *no longer deductible*. However, the meals around entertainment can be expensed, assuming these can be separated from the entertainment costs. Examples of entertainment expenses, which unfortunately are no longer deductible, include tickets to sporting events, rounds of golf, concert seats, and similar items.

Note about country clubs: A country club membership is *not* deductible because it's considered entertainment, but the meal and drink minimum portion could be if they or the membership serve a business purpose.

▶▶ ACTION ITEMS ◀◀

○ **Meal Expenses:** Be strategic and find ways to make the most of this expense. Keep detailed records of the meetings and the business purpose.

○ **Travel Expenses:** When you have travel plans, strategize to see if you can turn them into a deductible business trip. Keep detailed records of associated expenses and business activity.

CHAPTER 18

AUTOMOBILE EXPENSES

I f you have a business vehicle, there are some great tax savings strategies you can partake in. The cost of buying a car is just one part of the equation; many automobile expenses are deductible.

In this chapter, we'll cover this category thoroughly and explain what options and opportunities are available to you.

What Is a Business Vehicle?

A business vehicle is any type of automobile you use for business purposes. It can be driven by you, your employees, or both as long as it's primarily (more than 50%) used for business.

To claim tax deductions for everything from gas to repairs, you'll need thorough documentation of the vehicle's business use. You can't just slap a logo on a car and qualify for a deduction. You need to support and justify business use, as with any other deduction.

But before you choose a vehicle, you'll need to decide if you're going to buy or lease.

Buying vs. Leasing a Business Vehicle: Which Should You Choose?

When you're in the market for a business vehicle, one of the first things you're going to need to figure out is how you're going to pay for it. Will you buy it using cash, by taking out a loan, or by leasing it? Which one you choose affects how you calculate and deduct expenses.

Everyone's situation is different, so one option won't be universally better than the other. To help you figure out which one might be right for you, consider these questions:

- **How often do you expect to drive the vehicle (for both personal and business use)?** Leases have mileage limits. This might not be an issue if you don't plan to put a lot of miles on the vehicle, but it is something you should estimate upfront.

- **How many years do you plan on keeping the vehicle?** If you always want a new vehicle, leases can give you the flexibility to upgrade regularly.

- **How much do you want your monthly payment to be?** Lease payments are generally lower than loan payments, but you don't own a leased vehicle, so it isn't an asset.

When selling a purchased vehicle, you will have either a gain or a loss depending on the basis (Purchase Price less Depreciation). For example, say you purchased a $75,000 vehicle and depreciated all of it for a basis of $0. If you then sold it for $45,000, you would have a gain of $45,000 that you would have to pay some taxes on. This might not influence your decision between buying and leasing now, but it's important to keep in mind for the future.

Should I Put a Vehicle in My Personal or Business Name?

Once you've decided between buying and leasing, you'll want to decide whether to put the car in the business's name or your own. At the end of the day, either is acceptable. You just need to make sure you are following the correct process either way.

Personal Name

If you put the vehicle in your personal name and you are an S- or C-corp, you would use an accountable plan to reimburse yourself for the business use of the vehicle. If you are a sole proprietor or single-member LLC, you should include the business use in the Schedule C filing.

Business Name

If you end up having any personal use of the vehicle that is under the business, you would add that to your income as an employee (W-2) or an owner's draw. You can use the lease value rule. Under this rule, you determine the value of an automobile by using its annual lease value, which is provided by the IRS.

Generally, if the vehicle is 100% for business use, we would recommend using the business name to keep everything clean. But if the amount of business use is less than that, you can do whatever is easiest and most beneficial to you. Just remember to reimburse properly for your entity setup.

How To Calculate Automobile Deductions

There are two methods for calculating the business use of your vehicle to determine what to deduct: a mileage deduction method and an actual expenses method.

You must choose one. Here's how they compare:

Mileage Deduction

When you write off vehicle expenses using mileage, you deduct a certain amount per business mile. The tax deduction for business mileage changes every year.

There are pros and cons to this method, with the main advantage being that it's simple to do. But you can't deduct other expenses related to the vehicle (like maintenance, depreciation, repairs, gas, etc.). The idea behind the mileage deduction is that the annual per-mile rate covers those types of expenses and costs of owning the vehicle. You can still deduct parking, tolls, and interest expenses on the loan (if you purchased the vehicle).

Actual Expenses

The actual expense method is more precise but also more complicated.

For this option, you take the **business use percentage (BUP)** of the vehicle and multiply that by its **total actual expenses**. The calculation is simple:

Business Use Percentage (BUP) = Business Miles / Total Miles

Example: If you used your vehicle for a total of 15,000 miles in a year and your business miles were 12,000 of that, your BUP would be 80% (12,000 / 15,000).

Expenses can include loan interest (if owned), depreciation (if owned), lease payment (if leased), fuel, registrations, car washing, repairs and maintenance, insurance, and more. Once you've determined the total amount of vehicle expenses you've incurred in a given year, you multiply that number by your BUP to determine your total business tax deduction.

If you use the actual expense method, you cannot also take a mileage deduction. It is one or the other.

CHOOSING BETWEEN MILEAGE AND ACTUAL

When choosing between the mileage and actual methods, put a spreadsheet together to see which will give you a better deduction. This will vary depending on how you use the vehicle.

Note: You will typically use the mileage method if business use is less than 50%.

You can use the mileage or actual method whether you lease or purchase a vehicle, but there are items to consider for both.

- **Leased vehicles**
  - ° Once you pick a method, you have to stick with it for the life of the lease.
- **Purchased vehicles**
  - ° If you choose the actual method in year one, you must continue with that.
  - ° If you choose the mileage method in year one, you can switch to the actual method in future years but must use straight-line depreciation.

How Business Vehicle Depreciation Works

If you go the actual route for business vehicles, there are various depreciation options available, including:

- Straight-line depreciation.
- Bonus depreciation.
- Section 179 expensing.
- MACRS.

Depreciating a business vehicle has a lot to do with a vehicle's Gross Vehicle Weight Rating (GVWR). This represents how much a business vehicle weighs and how much it's capable of carrying, and it's used to determine which deductions you might qualify for.

When it comes to GVWR, you should know whether your vehicle is greater than or less than 6,000 pounds. Vehicles with a GVWR over 6,000 pounds may qualify for more favorable depreciation terms under Section 179 or bonus depreciation.

YEAR-END DEDUCTIONS

If you want the vehicle deduction for a car you purchased this year, you need to put it in service before the end of the year. "Put in service" means driving it at least one business mile before December 31.

Documentation for Automobile Expenses - Mileage Logs

First things first, a mileage log is *required*, even if you use a vehicle exclusively for business. There are a few options for keeping a mileage log. You can log:

- **Every day of the year:** Here, you would record every single mile you drive. You would have a list of which of those miles are business-related and which are personal. At the end of the year, you have total business versus personal mileage.

- **Three-month sample:** If your business activity is relatively consistent throughout the year, you can do a three-month sample where you do a full mileage log for three months (90 days) and apply that mileage and percentage to the entire year. This is our recommendation!

Of course, having a mileage log is just the first step. You also need documentation to support the actual business purpose of the miles as well. An easy way to do this is to record mileage right in your appointment book next to your meetings to support each trip.

EXAMPLE OF BUSINESS MILEAGE DOCUMENTATION

Let's say you have a client meeting at Starbucks. You'll have a mileage log to track the trip from the office to Starbucks, as well as a receipt from Starbucks with details describing the purpose of the meeting written on the back. You keep these documents together. This perfectly illustrates what you *should* be doing to record your business mileage and purpose.

Four Steps to Tax Planning for the Business Vehicle Deduction

If you haven't purchased a vehicle for business use yet, this is your opportunity to cash in on some serious tax savings for as long as you have that vehicle. Let's recap the four steps to choosing the right ride and tax planning for the biggest deduction:

- **First, decide if you're going to lease or purchase a vehicle.** You'll do this by considering use, the number of years you plan to use it, and your monthly budget.

- **Next, you'll put the vehicle in either your personal name or the business's name.** Consider whether it'll be mostly for business or personal use and the expected insurance premiums to choose the best option. Typically, we see higher insurance premiums when you put a vehicle in a business's name, but the difference isn't so significant that it should sway you one way or the other.

- **Choose either the mileage or the actual
  method to calculate your deduction.** You'll do
  this based on your use of the vehicle. If using the
  actual method, be sure to track all related expenses
  associated with the vehicle.

- **Keep a mileage log to prove the business use.**
  Even if the vehicle is only for business purposes, do
  this to cover your back in the event of an audit.

Always remember: The more after-tax dollars you turn into
pre-tax dollars, the more you save.

▶▶ ACTION ITEMS ◀◀

○ **Automobile Expenses:** Regardless of your business type, there is likely an automobile deduction you can take advantage of. Some businesses may see higher deductions than others, but don't overlook this valuable opportunity.

○ **Choose Your Method, Document, and Save:** Decide between the mileage or actual expense method to maximize your deduction, and keep an accurate, up-to-date mileage log. Retain all relevant documentation to support your chosen method.

CHAPTER 19

HIRING YOUR CHILDREN

Hiring your kids: Is it a good idea? Bad idea? Worth it? Not so much?

If you've considered hiring your kids to work for your business, give yourself a pat on the back for discovering one of the best-kept tax-saving secrets out there. Then, do it.

There's a common misconception that the IRS doesn't allow or approve of you hiring your kids. Not only is this not the case, but there are explicit rules allowing for this written in the tax code.

In this chapter, you'll learn what the IRS has to say about hiring your kids for your business and how to do so legally to reap the many benefits of having your children on payroll.

Why You Should Hire Your Kids

Hiring your kids can yield tax benefits, allowing them to potentially earn income tax-free.

According to the IRS:

> "Payments for the services of a child under age 18 who works for his or her parent in a trade or business are not subject to Social Security and

Medicare taxes if the trade or business is a sole proprietorship or a partnership in which each partner is a parent of the child."

In other words, if you pay your children through a sole proprietorship and they are under 18, neither you nor they need to pay Social Security, Medicare or FUTA taxes on those payments.

On top of that, your child can claim the standard deduction, so any income they make up to the standard deduction amount would be tax-free. That's a lot of tax-free income, and it will likely only go up each year!

On the business side, another benefit to hiring your kids is being able to deduct certain expenses you would likely pay for anyway. For example, if your child is an employee of your business, you can deduct things like a cell phone, leadership classes, and office space—as long as you can prove that they are used for business purposes.

This goes back to the concept of moving after-tax dollars to pre-tax dollars. Now, it's not as easy as simply paying your children and moving on. They need to be doing legitimate work for you, and you need to ensure you have solid documentation to back everything up. But when you do this, everybody wins.

How To Hire Your Children

Hiring your kids isn't complicated, but there are a few ways you can get into legal trouble if you're not careful about how you work or pay them. Make sure you're aware of the rules ahead of time if you're considering this.

RULES FOR HIRING CHILDREN

- **Kids must be age 7+.** This is an age that has been proven in tax court.
- **You must pay a reasonable wage.** Pay wages that are reasonable based on the child's age, experience, and task.
- **Track time.** Record how much work your child does to support the deduction the business takes.
- **Pay to an account in the child's name.** Your child's paycheck should not be deposited into an account you control.
- **Prepare a W-2 at year-end.**
- **Have required documentation.** You'll need a legitimate job description, employment agreement, hour/task tracking, proof of payment, etc.
- **Child labor laws still apply.** Don't abuse the situation by overworking your children.

Also, be sure to check in with your state and local laws to see if there is anything else you need to do to be compliant.

WHAT ABOUT S-CORPS?

If you operate as an S-corp, you're not considered a sole proprietorship or partnership, and you *would* need to withhold Social Security, Medicare, and other employer taxes from payroll payments, even if they are paid to your children. This would all be considered a business expense, so while you can deduct them when filing your taxes, this still reduces the amount of money your child(ren) receives each paycheck.

Solution: Family Management Company

If your business operates as an S-corp, there is one option to still allow for both you and your children to take advantage of significant tax savings: establishing a "family management company." This company would be set up as a sole proprietorship owned by you or your spouse and would employ your children. You can then have your S-corp pay the family management company for services performed by your children and pay your children through that company while avoiding Social Security and Medicare (since it operates as a sole proprietorship).

Non-Child Family Members

Yes, you're free to hire grandchildren, nieces, nephews, and other members of your family. However, only direct children can avoid Social Security and Medicare taxes. Still, this might be advantageous to your business in enough other ways to be more than worth it.

You can also use the "family management company" solution in this scenario. Let's imagine you wanted to hire your grandchildren while also avoiding the FICA taxes. You could have your child set up a sole proprietorship and offer services to your company. You would pay your child's sole proprietorship, and then your child's sole proprietorship could hire your grandchildren. This structure allows your child's business to employ your grandchildren, avoiding additional taxes.

Children Over 18: Shifting Employment Strategy

What about when your child turns 18? At this point, FICA exemptions no longer apply, so we suggest hiring them as independent contractors (1099) if it suits your business needs.

As a 1099 contractor, your child will be responsible for self-employment taxes, but here's the upside: those taxes apply only to their net profit. Now that they're an independent contractor, they can offset their earnings with a variety of deductions. Expenses like a home office, travel costs (to meet with their "client" – your business), and other legitimate business costs can lower their taxable income.

A note of caution: If your child's role closely resembles that of a typical employee (with tasks dictated by you, regular hours, etc.), you'll need to classify them as a W-2 employee to comply with IRS guidelines.

Hiring your kids is tax-smart, so you don't want to miss out on the benefits to both you and your kids. It's a great opportunity to potentially shift income from after-tax dollars to pre-tax dollars while helping your child grow their wealth tax-free!

▶▶ ACTION ITEMS ◀◀

○ **Hire Your Children:** If you have a child aged seven or older, find tasks they can handle within your business. This is one of my favorite strategies to help families maximize tax savings.

○ **Maintain Detailed Documentation:** Pay your child a fair wage aligned with industry standards, and track their work hours and tasks carefully. Deposit payments directly into an account in their name, issue the correct year-end forms, and keep all related records.

CHAPTER 20

TRADITIONAL VS. ROTH IRAS

Individual Retirement Accounts, commonly known as "IRAs," are your friend for retirement planning. They've been around and popular for a long time, and they're widely considered to be powerful retirement tools. However, one type of IRA, the Roth IRA, will always be the one we recommend first.

In this chapter, we'll talk about both traditional and Roth IRAs and explain why Roth IRAs should be favored as a business owner when you're planning for your personal retirement.

What Is a Traditional IRA?

A Traditional IRA is a tax-advantaged retirement account available to anyone with income. You do not need to open this plan through an employer.

With a traditional IRA, you contribute pre-tax earnings, and your account grows tax-free until you withdraw from it, making this a smart option for many. You can also qualify for a tax deduction on your contributions.

The contribution limit, or the amount you're allowed to contribute to this plan in any given year, changes annually. Plan holders in a higher age bracket are allowed to contribute more to "catch up" on their retirement planning. These are referred to as catch-up contributions.

Contributions

IRA contribution limits change annually and are per person. So, if you are married, your limit would be the yearly limit times two (based on qualifications).

Withdrawals

- You can begin withdrawing at age 59 ½.
- Withdrawals are taxed at your ordinary income tax rate at the time they are withdrawn.
- If you take an early withdrawal before retirement, you'll be hit with ordinary income tax along with a 10% penalty (unless certain rare circumstances are met).

Phase-Out

You can deduct traditional IRA contributions from your taxable income, but how much you're able to deduct depends on your personal income and filing status. It is also determined according to whether you are a participant or nonparticipant in an employer-sponsored retirement plan and if your spouse is as well. If you're married and both you and your spouse are participants, for example, you may not be eligible for the full deduction.

Adjusted limits for IRA deductions are often referred to as phase-out ranges. Here's how to tell if you can take the full deduction, partial deduction, or no deduction on your contributions.

- **Full deduction:** No phase-out if both you and your spouse are *not* participants in an employer plan or you are single.

° Deduct up to the full contribution limit.

° You may also be eligible for the full deduction if only one of you is covered by a plan and your adjusted gross income (AGI) is under a certain threshold.

- **Partial deduction:** Your maximum deduction starts to phase out (or is reduced) if you or your spouse are a participant in an employer plan and your AGI is between a certain range.

- **No deduction:** If your income is above a certain limit and either you or your spouse (or both of you) are participants, you will not be eligible to take any deduction on your contributions.

To see current annual limits, visit the IRS' website and search "IRA Deduction Limits."

What Is a Roth IRA?

Roth IRAs differ from traditional IRAs in that you get no deduction when contributing to the account, but your account grows tax-free. While you would pay taxes when withdrawing from a traditional IRA, you won't pay taxes later when you withdraw from a Roth.

Contributions

Contribution limits for Roth IRAs also change every year and are higher for people over the age of 50. Based on qualifications, you may be able to contribute over and above any 401(k) contribution limits to a Roth IRA.

Withdrawals

- You can begin withdrawing at age 59 ½.
- Roth IRAs have a five-year rule that requires you to wait at least five years after first contributing to a Roth IRA before making a withdrawal.

One reason you might choose a Roth IRA instead of a traditional IRA is if you think you'd save more by paying taxes now rather than in the future based on your earnings and income tax bracket. In other words, if you expect to make *less* money now than you will when you reach the age of 59 ½, you may be better off choosing a Roth IRA. For many business owners, a Roth IRA can offer significant tax-free growth, especially if they anticipate higher tax rates in retirement. But this is just one of many advantages of Roth over traditional. Let's talk about a few others.

Why Roth IRAs Are So Powerful

Compared to traditional IRAs, Roth IRAs offer more flexibility and better tax advantages. Here are just a few of the things that make these retirement accounts so powerful.

Distributions Are Tax-Free (Both Principal and Earnings)

Traditional IRAs allow you to deduct your contributions upfront but require you to pay taxes on your principal and earnings when withdrawing. Rather than get a tax deduction when contributing to a Roth IRA, you pay the taxes upfront but then enjoy tax-free growth and distributions. This can often lead to greater long-term savings, which is why many savvy savers choose Roths.

Withdraw Contributions (Not Earnings) Without Penalty

You can withdraw any contributions you previously made to your Roth IRA (A.K.A. principal) at any time without paying additional taxes or penalties. So, if you're strapped for cash, you can tap into your account.

Let's say you've contributed $6,000 per year (after tax) for four years to a Roth IRA. Eight years later, you hit a bind and need some cash. You can take the $24,000 you've contributed out of the IRA without paying any additional taxes or penalties on it. You just can't withdraw any earnings on the account until you hit the actual retirement age (59 ½)

No Required Minimum Distributions (RMDs)

With a traditional IRA (and many other retirement accounts), the government requires you to start taking minimum distributions from your savings at a certain age. These are required minimum distributions or RMDs.

You are not subject to RMDs with a Roth IRA and can leave your money alone for as long as you live if you so please.

Tax-Free Withdrawals for Large Investments

Roth accounts are great for investments from which you expect large returns because you are not paying any taxes on growth and future withdrawals.

This is also a good reason to self-direct your Roth IRA, so you can invest more aggressively and try to take advantage of this as a strategy. Earning 5% in a retirement account is great, but if you see an opportunity to earn 15% or 20% on something, a Roth IRA is a great source of investment funds.

Flexible Payment Account for Your Kids

If you decide to hire your kids, you could have them contribute their earnings to a Roth IRA. This allows them to access their funds when they need them while also getting a jump on saving for retirement.

What If You're Phased Out?

You may phase out of a Roth IRA, meaning you won't be able to contribute as much if you meet predetermined income levels. Depending on your income, you may be able to contribute less than the limit or not be able to contribute at all.

Fortunately, there is an option for high-income earners called a backdoor Roth IRA.

BACKDOOR ROTH IRAS

Backdoor Roth IRAs offer a completely legal way to work around phase-out limits for Roth IRAs with a simple conversion. Here are the steps:

- Open a traditional IRA and make a non-deductible contribution.
- Convert your traditional IRA to a Roth IRA.

That's it for phase-out limits. That said, the concept can be more complicated than this if you're starting with a deductible traditional IRA. Here are a couple of factors to consider:

- You can convert prior traditional IRA accounts to a Roth IRA, but you'll pay taxes on the value of the deductible traditional IRAs in the year of conversion.
- For deductible traditional IRA funds, you need to convert the pro rata portion of those, too, which could lead to a tax sting in that year if you had some prior accounts opened.

Either way, if you're planning on taking advantage of the backdoor Roth IRA strategy, reach out to your financial advisor and accountant to go through this, especially if you're starting with a prior deductible traditional IRA.

Whether you're a business owner or not, a Roth IRA is a great option for your retirement and tax planning. Though traditional IRAs do have their place, at TaxElm, we often recommend Roths to small business owners for their withdrawal advantages, tax benefits, and more.

▶▶ ACTION ITEMS ◀◀

○ **Traditional vs. Roth:** Decide which IRA type—
Traditional or Roth—best aligns with your financial
goals, and make contributions accordingly.

○ **Consider a Backdoor Roth:** If your income exceeds
Roth contribution limits, assess whether a backdoor
Roth IRA conversion is a good fit. If you have existing
pre-tax IRA funds, analyze whether a Roth conversion could be beneficial this year.

CHAPTER 21

RETIREMENT STRATEGIES

As a business owner, you have many retirement plan options to choose from besides IRAs, which can sometimes feel overwhelming.

In this chapter, I'll give an overview of different retirement strategy options and the tax benefits of each to help make this decision a little simpler.

Best Retirement Plans for Businesses Without Employees

If you own a business but don't have any employees (besides family members), you'll want to first ask yourself how much you want to put away each year. This will help determine which route to go.

- **A little:** Consider traditional or Roth IRAs for their accessibility and flexibility, but note that they have the lowest contribution limits.

- **More:** A SEP IRA may be the right fit for a moderate amount of savings, offering simplicity and higher contribution limits.

- **The most:** A solo 401(k) provides the highest contribution ceilings and the option for employer matching.

SEP IRA

A SEP IRA, which stands for a Simplified Employee Pension Plan IRA, is a retirement plan for small business owners and people who are self-employed. This plan is an uncomplicated option for people who want fuss-free retirement accounts.

Contributions

- Employee contributions are *not* allowed for a SEP IRA. Only the business may contribute to the retirement plan.

- If you *did* have employees, the business would have to contribute the same percentage of salary to *all* employees. That's why we don't recommend this option if you have employees.

- This plan allows the business owner to contribute up to 25% of their W-2 income. If you are a sole proprietor, the maximum is roughly 20% of net earnings up to the annual maximum.

Who Is This Plan for?

- Companies with few or no full-time employees.

- Business owners who are looking for a simple retirement plan.

- Employers who want to eliminate annual filings and compliance testing.

- Employers who don't mind contributing equally to all eligible participants.

SOLO 401(K)

A solo 401(k) is a self-employed retirement plan. On top of high limits, this plan offers advantages such as the option for a company to match your contributions and the choice of either pre-tax or Roth contributions.

Contributions

- **Limits:** For these plans, there is a maximum employee contribution, a maximum employer contribution, and a maximum combined contribution.
  - ° Contribution limits are several thousand dollars higher for people over the age of 50.

Who Is This Plan for?

- Solo entrepreneurs and employers with no full-time W-2 employees (only part-time).
- Highly successful solo entrepreneurs who are looking to make considerable contributions.
- Business owners who are thinking of adding employees in the future.
- Business owners who want to include their spouse in a retirement plan.

Retirement Plan Options
(No Employees)

Features	Traditional IRA	Roth IRA	SEP IRA	Solo 401k
Contribution Limit	Lowest	Lowest	Middle	Highest
Administration Required	No	No	No	Yes
Pre-Tax Contributions	Yes	No	Yes	Yes
Roth Available	No	Yes	Yes	Yes
IRS Filing Required	No	No	No	Yes

Best Retirement Plans for Businesses with Employees

Before you think about putting a retirement plan in place for your business with employees, it's important to establish why you think your business needs one. Typically, retirement plans are used in one or both of the following ways:

- You're an employer looking for your own retirement or tax savings.
- You're looking to help recruit and retain high-quality employees.

PAYROLL-DEDUCTED IRA

Payroll-deducted IRAs are IRAs set up by employees that use deductions from the employee's payroll as contributions. These are not employer-sponsored plans but offer a way for business owners to help their employees save for retirement.

Contributions

- **Limits:** Contribution limits for payroll-deducted IRAs change every year and are the same as those for traditional and Roth IRAs.
- Matching contributions from the employer are *not* allowed with this plan.
- Employees have a choice between pre-tax and Roth contributions.

Who Is This Plan for?

- Employers who want to offer a retirement plan without sponsoring the plan.

- Employers who do not plan to offer employer matching as a benefit.
- Employees who want the choice between pre-tax and Roth contributions.

SIMPLE IRA

SIMPLE IRAs are retirement plans that allow the choice of either pre-tax or Roth contributions. These are low-cost plans for employers that offer flexibility for both you and your employees. Only smaller businesses (under 100 participants) are eligible to participate in these plans.

Contributions

- **Employee limits:** Contribution limits for SIMPLE IRAs change every year.
    - ° The limit is several thousand dollars higher for people over the age of 50.
- **Employer limits:** A 3% match or 2% employer contribution is required with this plan.
- "Turn-key" matching and vesting options for easy compliance testing.
- Choice of employment qualification in the plan.
- There are no administration costs.

Who Is This Plan for?

- Companies with fewer than 100 participants in the plan.
- Business owners who don't mind an instant vesting schedule.

- Employers who are looking for a low-cost alternative to a 401(k) plan.
- Employers who want to eliminate annual filings and compliance testing.

SAFE HARBOR 401(K)S

A safe harbor 401(k) is a special type of 401(k) that is not subject to the same testing requirements and regulations as a typical 401(k). It is an employer-sponsored account that allows owners to maximize their contributions without relying on high employee contributions. These are very popular with small business owners looking to offer competitive retirement benefits.

Contributions
- **Limits:** For these plans, there is a maximum employee contribution, a maximum employer contribution, and a maximum combined contribution.

  ° Employers can contribute up to 25% to these plans.

  ° Contribution limits are several thousand dollars higher for people over the age of 50.

- "Turn-key" matching and vesting options for easy compliance testing.
- Both pre-tax and Roth options are available with this plan.

Who Is This Plan for?

- Companies with one or more full-time employees.

- Employers who want to maximize their own contributions.
- Businesses that are looking to compete for quality employees in their market.
- Employers who want to minimize annual compliance testing.

Note: A traditional 401(k) offers customization options but comes with more testing requirements. Traditional 401(k) plans are subject to annual nondiscrimination testing to ensure the benefits do not disproportionately favor highly compensated employees.

Retirement Plan Options
(with Employees)

Features	Payroll Deducted IRA	SIMPLE IRA	Safe Harbor 401(K)	Traditional 401(K)
Contribution Limit	Lowest	Middle	Highest	Highest
Administration Required	No	No	Yes	Yes
Pre-Tax Contributions	Yes	Yes	Yes	Yes
Roth Available	Yes	Yes	Yes	Yes
IRS Filing Required	No	No	Yes	Yes

Advanced Retirement Planning Options

If you've done all you can to contribute to a business retirement plan but are still looking to contribute more, you may consider a more customizable type of account, such as a cash balance plan or a non-qualified plan.

CASH BALANCE PLAN

A cash balance plan is a type of pension plan with defined employer contributions that are equal to a percentage of annual earnings. These plans can stand alone or be paired with any 401(k) or profit-sharing plan. They offer high contribution limits and substantial tax savings for business owners.

- **Limits:** This plan uses age-banded contribution rates to determine maximum contributions.
- All contributions are made by the employer.
- This plan has actuarial requirements in addition to normal compliance requirements.

NON-QUALIFIED PLANS

The term non-qualified plan describes a category of tax-deferred and employer-sponsored retirement plans that are an alternative to qualified plans such as traditional 401(k)s. They are non-qualified because they are exempt from testing requirements laid out in the Employee Retirement Income Security Act. Types of non-qualified plans include:

- Deferred compensation plans
- Bonus 162 plans or executive bonus plans
- Owner-only 401(k) plans

Non-qualified plans do not have the same contribution limits as qualified plans and they are typically used for highly compensated employees or executives. These plans do not provide the same tax benefits as qualified plans. With that being said, they do allow you to target certain individuals within a company without offering to everyone.

One of the main things to consider when choosing a plan for your business is what role you want to play in retirement planning and how competitive you want your employee benefits to be. Depending on your budget, the size of your business, and the needs and interests of your employees, you may choose a traditional option or an advanced retirement plan—there are no wrong answers.

▶▶ ACTION ITEMS ◀◀

○ **Business Without Employees?** Identify the best retirement option (such as a SEP IRA or Solo 401(k)), get it set up, and start funding it.

○ **Business With Employees?** Choose the right retirement plan for your team (Payroll-Directed IRA, SIMPLE IRA, Safe Harbor 401(k), or Traditional 401(k)), get it set up, and begin contributions.

○ **Already Maximizing Retirement?** Look into advanced retirement plan options to further increase contributions and tax benefits.

CHAPTER 22

DEDUCTING SELF-EMPLOYED HEALTH INSURANCE PREMIUMS

When you're self-employed, you get used to paying many of your expenses. That is why maximizing your deductions is so essential.

Health insurance can be a sizable monthly expense for small business owners. But if you're self-employed, you can deduct up to 100% of these premiums for you and your family. This chapter will focus on how this deduction works for different business types and the steps to take for maximum savings.

How To Qualify for the Self-Employed Health Insurance Deduction

To qualify for the self-employed health insurance deduction, you must meet two main requirements:

- **No other health coverage.** You can't claim this deduction if you're eligible for a health plan through your own or your spouse's employer.

- **Deduction limits based on income.** The

amount you can deduct for health insurance cannot exceed your business income.

Your entity setup determines the correct way to take this deduction.

How To Report Self-Employed Health Insurance Premiums as a Sole Proprietor or Single-Member LLC

As a sole proprietor or single-member LLC, deducting your self-employed health insurance premiums is simple.

Here's what to do and what not to do:

- **Do:** Deduct your self-employed health insurance on Schedule 1 (self-employed health insurance deduction) on your personal tax return (Form 1040).
- **Don't:** Take the deduction on your Schedule C.

Suppose you are set up as a partnership (not an S-corporation). In that case, you can either pay for your insurance personally and report it on Schedule 1 or, if the partnership pays for it, include it as a guaranteed payment on the partnership tax return and report it on Schedule 1.

How To Report Self-Employed Health Insurance Premiums as an S-Corporation Owner

The process is a little more complicated for S-corps and LLCs taxed as S-corps. You must take a few additional steps to ensure you get the full deduction for your premiums as the owner. You might remember reading about these in **Chapter 6: S-Corp Requirements and Deductions**.

To briefly recap, the steps are:

- **Deduct the insurance as a business expense.**
- **Record the insurance payments as payroll.**
- **Deduct the payments on your personal tax return.**

It is important to note that this treatment is only for S-corp owners. You would not use this strategy for the rest of your employees if you have any.

How To Report Insurance Premiums Paid for Non-Owner Employees

If you have employees for whom you provide health insurance benefits (either partly or wholly), you can deduct these costs. All you must do is include the amount on each employee's W-2 in Box 12 with code DD. *This approach only applies to non-owner employees.*

Note: Depending on how many employees you have, you may be required to offer health insurance as a benefit. Remember this for your future tax planning, even if you're not giving your employees insurance now or don't have employees.

Health Share Plans

Medical sharing plans are not technically considered health insurance and are therefore not deductible through the business.

Deducting your health insurance premiums is just one way to save on taxes. However, as you know, insurance costs are only part of the puzzle when it comes to medical expenses. Next, we'll dive into health savings accounts.

▶▶ ACTION ITEMS ◀◀

○ **Utilize the Self-Employed Health Insurance Deduction:** If you are self-employed and paying for health insurance, you more than likely qualify. Ensure you properly take the deduction based on your specific entity type.

CHAPTER 23

HEALTH SAVINGS ACCOUNTS (HSAS)

When it comes to healthcare, a health savings account (HSA) can play an important role in softening the blow of significant expenses—but not everyone will qualify to open one. Consider this when choosing insurance for yourself and your employees, and understand how these savings accounts work for tax planning and budgeting.

What Is an HSA?

An HSA is a special type of savings account used for health-related expenses. You contribute pre-tax money to it and use the funds to pay for qualified medical expenses such as:

- Insurance deductibles and copays.
- Prescriptions and treatments.
- Mobility aids, hearing aids, vision aids, etc.
- Home health care items.
- Approved medical equipment like blood pressure monitors, support braces, first aid, etc.
- Other medically necessary expenses.

If you withdraw money from an HSA for non-medical expenses, you'll face a 20% penalty plus taxes (with some exceptions for those over a certain age).

Unlike a flexible spending account (FSA), which enforces a "use it or lose it" rule, an HSA allows funds to roll over year after year.

HSA CONTRIBUTION LIMITS

Every year, the contribution limits for individual and family HSAs change.

Six Key Benefits of an HSA

An HSA is a powerful tool with a number of unique benefits. Here are a few of the main advantages of these accounts:

- **Contributions are deductible.** Traditionally, you must itemize deductions for out-of-pocket health costs to get a tax benefit. With an HSA, you deduct contributions.

- **Withdrawals are tax-free.** If used for qualified medical expenses, HSA withdrawals are not taxed.

- **Interest and earnings are *not* taxed.** Your contributions grow tax-free until you use them.

- **HSAs can be self-directed.** You can invest HSA funds in mutual funds, stocks, rental properties, etc. These accounts don't have to grow at a traditional savings rate.

- **You choose when to use it.** This is not a use it or lose it account. Your contributions will be there when you need them and will not disappear.

- **Accounts are portable.** You can change employers or retire and keep an HSA.

The IRS doesn't often let you "win" on both the contribution and the withdrawal, so you can probably see why we recommend everyone (business owner or not) max out their HSA contributions if they qualify.

Am I Eligible To Contribute to an HSA?

We mentioned earlier that not just anyone can open and use an HSA. To be eligible, you must meet these qualifications:

- **You're covered by a high-deductible health insurance plan (HDHP).**
    - ° See the IRS website for minimum deductible requirements for any given year.
- **You're not covered by any other plan that is not an HDHP.**
- **You're not eligible for Medicare.**
- **You have not been claimed as a dependent on someone else's return.**

Although a high deductible might typically turn you away from an insurance plan, HSA eligibility could be a good reason to reconsider.

Why HSAs Are Always a Good Idea

An HSA is one of the few tools that allows you to make tax-deductible contributions and withdraw funds tax-free. For this reason, anyone eligible to take advantage of this powerful tax-saving vehicle should consider it. Even if you're healthy now and unlikely to use the funds soon, the sooner you start saving, the better prepared you'll be in the future.

And when high medical costs happen, let's talk more about what you can do to care for them.

▶▶ ACTION ITEMS ◀◀

○ **Maximize and Invest Your Contributions:** If eligible, aim to maximize your HSA contributions each year. Treat it like another retirement plan with tax-free benefits going in and coming out. Consider investing any funds you don't immediately need for medical expenses to grow your HSA balance over time.

CHAPTER 24

MEDICAL EXPENSE REIMBURSEMENT - SECTION 105 PLANS

When medical expenses hit, even the best insurance and HSAs may not cover everything. Enter the Section 105 Plan—a powerful tax-saving strategy that converts personal medical costs into business deductions, designed for business owners without other employees.

This chapter will cover how small business owners can save on medical expenses with a Section 105 reimbursement plan. Find out if you qualify for this tax strategy and how to implement it.

What Is a Section 105 Plan?

A Section 105 plan enables personal medical expenses to be converted into business deductions. This is a type of medical reimbursement plan or health reimbursement arrangement that allows qualifying business owners to deduct qualifying health expenses for themselves as employees.

This plan is particularly advantageous for those with consistently high out-of-pocket medical costs.

HOW TO QUALIFY FOR A SECTION 105 PLAN

Section 105 plans are for business owners without employees other than themselves and their spouses. To be eligible, you must meet two requirements:

- **You have only one employee.** This would either be you, if you're single, or your spouse.
- **You operate your business as one of the following:**
  - Sole proprietorship (Schedule C).
  - Partnership (Form 1065).
  - Rental property (Schedule E).
  - C-corporation (Form 1120).

If operating as a sole proprietor, the tax law does not consider you an employee of your business, which is why you need to hire your spouse. And if you do hire your spouse, they must actually work for your business to justify receiving medical reimbursements.

WHEN A SECTION 105 PLAN DOESN'T MAKE SENSE

Here are a few circumstances in which Section 105 planning is not a viable option.

S-Corps

S-corps do not qualify for a Section 105 Plan, so you'll need to consider a workaround if your business is an S-corp. This could entail separating a part of your business away from the S-corp and into a sole proprietorship (if married) or a C-corporation (if single).

Business with Other Employees

If you have other employees in your business, you would not qualify for a Section 105 plan. You would instead need to look at other HRA options, which we'll discuss in **Chapter 25: Health Strategies for Businesses with Employees**.

Multiple Businesses

If you have multiple businesses, you would need to count all employees in all of your businesses. Therefore, you would not qualify for a Section 105 unless there were no employees, which isn't likely.

How To Create a Section 105 Plan

It's important to ensure your Section 105 plan is set up correctly. Otherwise, reimbursements could be deemed invalid.

The plan must be formally documented and include:

- Defined allowances for medical expenses.
- Specified periods of coverage.
- Provisions for reimbursement and exclusions.

Note: Even if you're the only employee at your company, your Section 105 must be formally written to be compliant.

Single

If you're single, you would need to be operating your business (or part of your business) as a C-corporation to qualify for a Section 105 plan.

Married

If you're married, you can hire your spouse as your only employee. This plan would include reimbursement for expenses incurred by:

- The employee (your spouse).
- The employee's spouse (you).
- The employee's dependents (your children).
- Any children of the employee under age twenty-seven.

With your Section 105 plan in place, you would turn medical expenses into deductible business expenses and record these as "employee welfare benefits" for tax purposes.

To show the impact this could make, let's say you are operating your business as a sole proprietor and you have high medical costs. You could hire your spouse in your business and implement a Section 105 plan to reimburse your employee (your spouse) and their family (you and your children). If you have $20,000 in medical expenses and are in the 24% tax bracket, by setting up a Section 105 plan, you would be saving over $4,800 in taxes. Keep in mind, that is before considering possible state taxes.

If you are in an unfortunate situation where you are facing high medical costs, a Section 105 plan can be a glimpse of light during these hard times. It can bring with it an opportunity for you to move after-tax spending into pre-tax spending by getting a business deduction for personal medical expenses. The next chapter will dive into strategies for businesses with employees, expanding on health cost savings beyond the individual business owner.

▶▶ ACTION ITEMS ◀◀

○ **High Medical Expenses?** If you incur significant out-of-pocket medical costs each year, consider setting up a Section 105 plan to help offset those expenses.

○ **If Applicable, Correctly Implement:** Create a formal written plan and keep detailed records of all reimbursements, including eligible expenses, proof of payment, and required employee documentation.

CHAPTER 25

HEALTH STRATEGIES FOR BUSINESSES WITH EMPLOYEES

You're a small business owner looking to grow and hire employees. You understand that to find and retain quality talent, you need to offer quality benefits. Health insurance is a great place to start.

This chapter is for small businesses with fewer than 50 employees that want to offer health benefits. Many owners feel that traditional group health plans are too costly, but there are alternatives worth considering. Health reimbursement arrangements (HRAs) and qualified small employer HRAs (QSEHRAs) offer flexible, tax-efficient solutions that can provide quality benefits without stretching your budget. In this chapter, we'll dive into these options to help you decide if they're a good fit for your employee benefits package.

What Is a Health Reimbursement Arrangement (HRA)?

A health reimbursement arrangement (HRA) is an IRS-approved, employer-funded health benefit used to reim-

burse employees for out-of-pocket medical expenses and insurance.

HRAs have a fixed cost and allow you to give employees tax-free money to purchase insurance independently. You set a monthly benefit allowance to cover eligible medical expenses such as:

- Medication.
- Treatment.
- Medical equipment.
- Hospital visits.
- Diagnostic testing.

Some items are eligible for reimbursement automatically and some require a prescription or doctor's note. Others are not eligible for reimbursement at all.

Why an HRA? Traditional group health benefits are often expensive and complex to manage, so many business owners look to HRAs as a simple and cost-effective way to offer health benefits to employees. And while similar to simply paying your employees more, payments to an HRA are not taxed, saving both of you money.

How To Set up an HRA

Setting up an HRA involves a few straightforward steps that outline what you, the employer, need to do and how employees can apply for reimbursement:

- **The employer sets the allowance.** Start by deciding on the tax-free amount you'll offer each employee monthly, keeping in mind the yearly maximum limits.

- **Employees purchase healthcare.** Employees then use their own funds to purchase the healthcare products or services they choose.

- **Employees submit proof of expenses.** To get reimbursed, employees provide proof of their eligible expenses. This documentation typically includes a description of the product or service, cost, purchase date, and a doctor's note or prescription if required.

- **Employer reviews documents and reimburses expenses.** Once you confirm the expense is eligible, you approve and reimburse up to the set allowance.

Note: These reimbursements are free from payroll tax for both the business and the employee. They're also exempt from income tax for employees with a qualifying health insurance plan.

What Is a Qualified Small Employer HRA (QSEHRA)?

A QSEHRA is a specialized HRA available to employers with fewer than 50 full-time employees who don't offer group health insurance.

With this arrangement, you can reimburse employees tax-free for medical expenses (including health insurance premiums) up to an annual allowance limit.

Every employee must receive the same allowance unless a family status change justifies a different limit. All full-time employees are eligible, but you can also choose to include part-time staff.

QSEHRAs can be offered alongside HSAs. If you have more than 50 employees, you may want to look at an Individual Coverage HRA (ICHRA) or Group Coverage HRA (GCHRA) instead.

Health Care Sharing Ministry

Employees enrolled in a health care sharing ministry can have eligible expenses reimbursed through the QSEHRA. However, since it's not health insurance, all reimbursements are subject to income tax. Any membership fees associated with the sharing plan aren't eligible for reimbursement.

How To Set up and Manage a QSEHRA

Starting or switching to a QSEHRA is simple when you follow these steps:

Setting up a QSEHRA

- Choose a start date and, if necessary, cancel any existing group policy.
- Verify which employees are eligible for the benefit.
- Determine your budget and set allowances for employees.
- Prepare legal plan documents and establish procedures.
- Communicate the benefit details to employees and provide resources for purchasing individual health insurance.

Each step should align with your state's QSEHRA deadlines to ensure compliance.

Managing a QSEHRA

- Keep benefits updated, track changes in regulations, and adjust allowances as needed.
- Process reimbursements efficiently and maintain documentation.

- Consider self-administering, hiring a third-party administrator (TPA), or using a software provider to handle the administration with ease.

Four Benefits of HRAs and QSEHRAs

Offering group health insurance and increasing employee wages may be fine for many companies, but there's much to like about HRAs and QSEHRAs compared to these options. Here are a few key advantages we explain to employers choosing health benefits.

Allows Employers To Set Allowance Caps

You, the employer, are in complete control of the costs for these arrangements. Once the caps are set, they cannot be exceeded.

Avoids Group Health Insurance Qualification

Group health insurance can be complex. Re-enrollment and premium increases are headaches for many employers and are always challenging to plan for. With an HRA, you know what to expect and can continue giving your employees competitive benefits with less hassle.

Gives Employees Flexibility

Employees can choose how they want to use their allowance, whether on health insurance premiums, out-of-pocket expenses, or both.

Helps Attract and Retain Employees

Talented employees look for good benefits. Offering an HRA can help you attract the right people to positions at your company and make them far more likely to stick around.

Hopefully, it's crystal clear why so many small business owners like HRAs. At TaxElm, we recommend these as part of not only your tax-planning strategy but also your strategy for growing your business with great employees.

▶▶ ACTION ITEMS ◀◀

○ **Already Offering Health Benefits?** Complete a review of your current employee health benefits and confirm they still meet your budget and needs.

○ **Not Currently Offering Benefits?** Review the options available and implement a strategy that works for your business.

CHAPTER 26

BUSINESS CREDITS

When we talk about various business deductions we talk about how they are often the result of an incentive that the government is giving us because they want something. This is the same when it comes to business tax credits. Tax deductions lower your taxable income, but tax credits reduce your actual tax owed, dollar-for-dollar. This direct reduction in taxes makes tax credits extremely attractive.

The government offers all sorts of different tax credits, including items associated with hiring, innovation, energy, research, etc. This chapter is going to specifically dig into two common business tax credits: the Work Opportunity Tax Credit and the Research and Development Tax Credit.

Work Opportunity Tax Credit (WOTC)

The WOTC is a federal general business tax credit available to employers who hire individuals from specific targeted groups that have been faced with employment challenges. This credit rewards your good deeds and opens doors for people who may have been overlooked in the job market.

Eligibility Criteria

Employers who hire an individual who is part of a targeted group may qualify for the WOTC. The targeted group includes qualified veterans, recipients of certain public assistance programs, ex-felons, individuals living in designated community zones, vocational rehabilitation referrals, summer youth employees, Supplemental Nutrition Assistance Program (SNAP) recipients, Supplemental Security Income (SSI) recipients, and long-term family assistance recipients.

Claiming the Credit

To properly claim this credit, there are a few steps that need to occur. First, the employee and employer must complete a pre-screening form to confirm that the employee falls into one of the targeted groups mentioned above. This pre-screening form must be submitted to a local agency within 28 days of the employee being hired. The local agency will certify that the employee is eligible which will then allow the business to claim the credit on their business tax return.

Research and Development (R&D) Tax Credit

The R&D tax credit is designed to reward companies that engage in qualifying research activities. Its purpose is to drive innovation and advance technology across various sectors.

Qualifying Activities

Many people think R&D involves scientists or people in a lab mixing different chemicals, but it actually covers a much broader scope. We see this tax credit apply to companies in industries such as manufacturing, software development, food and beverage, consulting, and more.

Qualifying activities for the R&D tax credit include developing new or enhanced products, processes, or software. To meet eligibility, the research must rely on scientific or technical principles and seek to resolve uncertainty about how something functions or is designed. There needs to be a process of experimentation involved.

Claiming the Credit

To properly claim this credit, you need to have strong documentation of the various phases of your research and development efforts. The credit is based on qualifying expenditures during the development, which includes wages (for those working on, supervising, or supporting the process), supplies (items used during the process), and contract research (outside vendors brought in to help with the process).

If you are looking to take full advantage of the R&D tax credit, we recommend working with an expert. There are specific things that the IRS is looking for, and specialists can help organize everything for you to ensure you are getting the most out of the credit.

Remember, tax credits are dollar-for-dollar reductions in your taxes. The government will not come knocking on your door forcing you to take advantage of these credits, it is your responsibility to research which ones may apply to you and then put them to work. These are just two of the most common tax credits we see being used by TaxElm members, but there are hundreds out there.

▶▶ ACTION ITEMS ◀◀

○ **Identify Eligible Credits:** Review your business activities to determine if you qualify for credits like the Work Opportunity Tax Credit (WOTC) or the Research and Development (R&D) Credit.

○ **Research Other Tax Credits:** There are many government credits available to small businesses. Many of them are industry-specific. Do your research to see if your specific industry and business may qualify for the other tax credits available.

CHAPTER 27

REAL ESTATE TAXES

ental property investments are not for the faint of heart. They're more intimidating than other assets because they come with many nuances and challenges. But they also offer many opportunities to save on taxes if you play your cards right and know where to look for advantages.

In this chapter, we're going to cover a lot of ground, including the following topics:

- Depreciation and how it works for rental properties.
- Repairs, improvements, and maintenance.
- Losses and how to use them to your advantage.
- Active investors and real estate professionals.
- Deductible expenses for rental investments.

We'll wrap up with some tax-saving strategies for rental property owners. Let's get into it.

How Does Depreciation Work for Rental Real Estate?

We have some good news for anyone looking to purchase rental real estate.

Everything can be depreciated in a rental property investment except for raw land. This includes buildings, flooring, appliances, sinks, driveways, landscaping, and more.

One advantage of investing in real estate is that for many of the early years, you often have a positive cash flow but show a loss (for tax purposes), and this is due to depreciation. Who wouldn't want to bring in cash without paying taxes on it?

But to depreciate properly, you need to know the value of your land.

HOW TO DETERMINE LAND VALUE TO MAXIMIZE DEPRECIATION

To take advantage of what you can depreciate, you must first identify what you *can't* depreciate. Basically, you must find the value of the raw land versus everything else. **The goal is to assign as much value as possible to the building and improvements.**

The IRS recommends using the local property tax assessment to determine land value, but you can also use your own appraisal or replacement cost to do this as long as you have a reasonable basis to back up the allocation.

DEPRECIATION RECAPTURE TAX

We're about to talk about just how much you can save with depreciation, but it's important to be aware of the costs associated with this, too. If/when you decide to sell an asset that has been depreciated, you will need to pay a depreciation recapture tax.

This means that although you get a great write-off from the depreciation, you may need to pay it back someday down the road. However, with the time value of money factored in, not to mention potential exit strategies to defer or eliminate the gain, we almost always recommend taking advantage of as much depreciation as possible.

Depreciable Life for a Real Estate Investment

Generally speaking, you would depreciate over 27.5 years for residential property or 39 years for nonresidential property. But these figures are only for the structure itself. Other parts of the property can be depreciated sooner, which you'll want to do.

- **Personal property**: five or seven years
- **Land improvements**: 15 years
- **Structure**: 27.5 years (residential) or 39 years (nonresidential)

As you can see, you can pull certain costs into land improvements and personal property to depreciate expenses sooner and reduce your taxable income earlier in the investment.

This is called cost segregation, and you can use it to take more write-offs.

What Is a Cost Segregation Study?

When you purchase a property, you're dealing with a building structure as well as all of its interior and exterior components. Often, this works in your favor as the owner.

Typically, 20% to 40% of these components fall into tax categories that allow for faster write-offs compared to the building structure.

A cost segregation study breaks down the construction costs or purchase price of the property, which would normally be depreciated over 27.5 or 39 years.

The main objective is to pinpoint all costs related to the property that can be depreciated over shorter periods, such as five, seven, or 15 years.

Typically, a cost segregation study is most advantageous for multi-family and commercial properties and less for single-family rentals.

How To Carry out a Cost Segregation Study

You'll follow these three steps to perform a cost segregation study:

- **Divide land between raw land and land improvements**. The more you get into land improvements, the more you can depreciate over 15 years.

- **Divide the building into the structure and personal property**. The more you get into personal property, the more you can depreciate over five to seven years.

- **Depreciate the rest accordingly.** Depreciate remaining structure items over the typical 27.5 or 39 years—the raw land, of course, can't be depreciated.

These studies are complicated, so we recommend working with a professional here.

BONUS DEPRECIATION AND COST SEGREGATION

Remember when we talked about the advantages of bonus depreciation for saving more on taxes in year one? This applies to rental real estate as well. Bonus depreciation allows you to depreciate more in qualified property in the first year, which can be very advantageous for some small business owners. Qualified property includes items with a useful life of 20 years or less.

When we look at the cost segregation study above, we can utilize bonus depreciation for items we could pull away from the structure to get more depreciation in year one.

Note: There is a percentage limit to how much of an item's cost you can deduct with bonus depreciation. Just be aware of this.

Rental Property Depreciation Example

To show you how rental property depreciation works in practice, look at this example.

- **You purchased a multi-family rental in 2022 and spent:**
- **$500,000 in total costs:**
  - **$100,000 allocated to land**
  - **$400,000 allocated to the building**

In this example, the $100,000 allocated to land cannot be depreciated. And without cost segregation or bonus depreciation, you'd depreciate the remaining $400,000 for the building over 27.5 years. This would be roughly $18,000 in depreciation per year.

But let's assume you do decide to do a cost segregation study and can pull 30% of the building cost and move it into five-, seven-, or 15-year property. That would be $120,000. And with 100% bonus depreciation available in 2022, you could have depreciated the full $120,000 in year one with the remaining $280,000 over 27.5 years.

To recap:

First-year depreciation:

- **$18,000** with traditional methods
- **$130,000** with a cost segregation study + bonus depreciation (based on 2022 numbers)

Real Estate Repairs/Maintenance vs. Improvements

Now that you're clear on depreciating purchase costs, it's time to discuss how to save on ongoing costs.

There's a big difference between repairs and improvements in real estate, and this difference is important in your tax planning. At the end of the day, you expense repairs immediately but capitalize and depreciate improvements.

REAL ESTATE REPAIRS AND MAINTENANCE

Repairs and maintenance keep your property in normal operating condition. These items do not materially add value to your rental or prolong its life.

Repairs and maintenance could include:

- Painting.
- Repairing flooring.
- Fixing leaky plumbing.
- Repairing appliances.

The great thing about repairs and maintenance is that you can expense them immediately without worrying about depreciation or depreciation recapture.

REAL ESTATE IMPROVEMENTS

Improvements add value to your property and/or are intended to prolong its life. Improvements go beyond repairs.

Improvements could include:

- Additions (deck, new room, etc.).
- Entire room renovations.
- New windows.
- New appliances.
- Landscaping.

If an item falls under the category of improvements, you need to capitalize the costs and depreciate. Again, this also makes an expense subject to depreciation recapture when you sell.

THREE TYPES OF IMPROVEMENTS

To further clarify the difference between repairs and improvements, the tax law defines three main types of improvements.

- **Betterment:** Increases a property's value, efficiency, strength, or quality.
- **Restoration**: Returns a property to its ordinary condition after it has fallen into a state of disrepair or after its class life.
- **Adaption**: Converts a property into something different (new use).

Three Ways To Turn Spending into Repairs

In general, repairs benefit you more than improvements for saving purposes because you can expense these immediately and avoid depreciation. This is why you may want to do a bit of pre-planning to avoid any improvement expenses you don't need to be paying.

Separate Repairs from Improvements

Request separate invoices for repairs and improvements so you can expense as many repairs as possible. To do this, make sure your contractors label items as either repairs or improvements *or* use separate contracts/contractors for these.

Repair vs. Replace

Avoid replacing items that don't strictly need replacing in favor of fixing them. Examples include:

- Restore flooring in your rental rather than ripping it up.
- Repair windows before putting in new ones.
- Fix appliances that break instead of replacing them.

Use Similar Materials

Being consistent about which materials you use for repairs can help you keep what you need on hand to save on future maintenance. This also simplifies your expensing.

Overall, it's important to put your spending on rental properties into the right categories and to prioritize repairing over improving.

What You Need To Know About Real Estate Losses

Real estate rental properties often produce losses. Why is this?

Essentially, it's because of depreciation and expenses. Rental properties often have positive cash flow—money in your pocket—

but show a loss on paper because of the high depreciation you can take early on. You also have regular operating expenses, over and above depreciation, helping to increase this loss. Losses from real estate are considered "passive losses."

How Passive Losses Are Handled

The biggest downfall of passive activity is limitations on what it can be used to offset.

Passive losses can only offset other passive income. You can't use a passive loss to offset earned income, capital gains (unless from passive activity), or portfolio income.

Essentially, if you have a rental property (passive) with a loss due to high depreciation, you can only offset that loss against other passive income (rental activity or businesses you don't actively participate in). You can't use it to offset W-2 income, business income, or non-passive capital gains.

UNUSED PASSIVE LOSSES

If you have passive losses but not enough passive income to offset them, these losses don't just disappear.

Unused passive losses (A.K.A. suspended losses) can be carried forward to future years when you may have passive income *or* when you sell a rental property for a gain.

So, when you can't use a passive loss right away, know that you will eventually be able to.

How To Utilize Passive Losses

Here are some strategies to maximize passive losses.

Be an Active Real Estate Investor

If you're under certain income limits and are actively involved in managing your property, you may qualify as an active investor. Being an active investor allows you to deduct up to $25,000 in rental real estate losses. We're going to cover this shortly.

Become a Real Estate Professional

Qualifying as a real estate professional lets you fully deduct passive losses against your ordinary income. There are various requirements you need to meet, but we'll get to those.

Generate More Passive Income

This one has to do with making the most of distinct entities. Some questions to ask yourself:

- If there's part of your business you don't actively participate in, could you split it off into a separate passive entity?
- Do you have another property you could sell at a gain to use the losses against?
- Do you have a highly appreciated asset you could sell at a gain to use the losses against?
- Can you invest in a high-cash-flow passive activity that the losses can be used to offset?

You may need to do some planning and adjusting to qualify for a certain status or generate more passive income.

Active Investors and Real Estate Professionals

Real estate is tricky and usually treated much differently than a typical business.

As we have just started to cover, maximizing losses has a lot to do with your status, and you can save more as an active investor or real estate professional. But what do these terms mean?

ACTIVE REAL ESTATE INVESTORS

Active real estate investors get better tax breaks because the IRS believes they need them more.

If you "actively participate" in managing a rental property, you can utilize up to $25,000 in rental real estate losses to offset other income—including ordinary income. To be considered an active participant, there are income limits and requirements you need to meet.

These are:

- **Your AGI (adjusted gross income) must be under $100,000.**

    ° The deduction starts to phase out for income between $100,000 and $150,000 and is completely phased out over $150,000.

- **You need to "actively participate" or have some hands-on involvement in managing the property.** This requirement is easy to meet.

    ° Participation doesn't need to be regular, continuous, or substantial to count and can be as simple as making management decisions or hiring contractors for services.

Anyone who can qualify should be shooting for active real estate investor status because it's easy to achieve and lets you deduct far more in losses.

If your income phases you out of active status, you might want to be a real estate professional.

What Is a Real Estate Professional?

Like active investors, real estate professionals enjoy greater loss deductions. However, real estate professionals must meet stricter requirements and are often more heavily involved in their investments.

As a real estate professional, you can offset ordinary income with rental losses and use your *full* loss (you're not limited to $25,000). To qualify as a real estate professional, you need to materially participate and pass two additional tests.

REAL ESTATE PROFESSIONAL REQUIREMENTS

The IRS requires investors to meet one of seven initial activity tests to qualify for *material participation*. Most likely, you'll meet one of these two:

- You participated in the activity for more than 500 **hours for the year**.

- You participated in the activity for more than 100 **hours**, *and* **you participated more than any other individual for the year** (including individuals who didn't own interest).

If you pass this first test, there are two more requirements to qualify as a *real estate professional*. You must meet both:

- You performed more than **750 hours of services** during the tax year in real property trades or businesses in which you materially participated.

- **More than half of your working hours for the year** were in the real estate in which you materially participated.

Understand that **you must both materially participate _and_ meet the real estate professional tests to qualify as a real estate professional.** These activities are separate.

However, you can elect to treat all of your real estate activities as a single activity. This would be helpful if you can't meet the 750-hour requirement for any single activity or you don't meet the material participation test in an activity for which you want to use the losses.

Qualifying as a real estate professional is complex and requires detailed documentation. Be sure to take this seriously and keep your eyes on the prize (being able to offset earned income with rental losses!).

Example of Active Investor vs. Real Estate Professional

Rental activity is typically passive, meaning you can usually only offset other passive income with it. But with active investor or real estate professional status, you can offset ordinary income, too.

To demonstrate how these two options compare and why it's beneficial to strive for them, take a look at this example with the same income and losses:

Assumptions

- **W-2 or business income:** $90,000
- **Rental losses:** $70,000 (due to high initial depreciation and normal operating expenses)

Active Investor

If you actively participate in the rental activity by meeting the two requirements we outlined, you could take $25,000 worth of losses to offset a portion of your W-2 or business income and carry forward the rest. This means you only need to pay taxes on $65,000 of your income.

Note: If you did not actively participate, you wouldn't be able to use the passive losses until you had passive income. But if you do qualify, we recommend taking advantage right away.

Real Estate Professional

If you qualified as a real estate professional *and* materially participated in the activity, you could take the full $70,000 loss against your W-2 or business income. This means you would only pay taxes on $20,000.

Utilizing real estate losses is a great way to cut your tax bill. Just be sure you're doing it correctly and documenting everything thoroughly to keep more of your earnings.

Rental Property Deductions

There are many normal operating expenses associated with owning rental properties. This is a given. But what's not a given are the many tax-saving opportunities beyond depreciation and these normal expenses.

Think about your rental property expenses as you do business expenses. If you have valid deductions, you should be taking them. Your focus should be on maximizing the advantages available to you.

And if you remember from our chapter on business expenses (**Chapter 13: Maximizing Deductions**), expenses must be ordinary and necessary to be deductible. You'll recall:

- **Ordinary** = Common and accepted in the industry
- **Necessary** = Appropriate and required or helpful in operating

An ordinary and necessary expense is appropriate and helpful for your rental property. Expenses don't have to be frequent or recurring to count, but they can be.

Examples of Deductible Rental Property Expenses

There are *many* ordinary and necessary expenses for rental real estate. Some of the most common expenses include:

- Advertising.
- Cleaning.
- Depreciation.
- Insurance.
- Lawn care/exterior upkeep.
- Mortgage interest.
- Property management fees.
- Property taxes.
- Repairs and maintenance (see section above).
- Travel (to check in on property).
- Utilities.

This is not an exhaustive list, but a good place to start.

We've said it before and we'll say it again: Back up any and all expenses with documentation. Write on your receipts, take pictures, and store them digitally for future use.

Three Expense Planning Opportunities

Aside from knowing what you can deduct and keeping rock-solid records, there are more things you can do to plan around expenses and unlock more savings.

Hire Your Spouse To Manage the Property

Assuming you're a sole owner, you can hire your spouse for property management and deduct even more expenses. Retirement contributions, high medical costs, and more could qualify for deductions.

Hire Your Children To Manage the Property

It's no secret I feel strongly that hiring your children is one of the best tax strategies out there. This holds true for rental properties.

When you hire your children to help out with property management, you can get a deduction, and your children can potentially pay no taxes on their income. You're going to support them anyway, right? Why not get a tax advantage for it?

Set up Your Own Management Company

Setting up a management company makes sense if you want to take advantage of a particular retirement plan or benefit. You can't fund a solo 401(k) or a SEP IRA with a typical rental property, but you could fund these accounts if you had a management company.

This strategy makes even more sense when you manage properties other than your own. But if you don't fit into these categories, don't use this method.

You're leaving this chapter with a lot more information about rental real estate and taxes than you came with. You can see there are many tax benefits available that require varying levels of planning and hoop-jumping. But if you own real estate, you're probably up to the challenge.

Next, we want to put a spotlight on a specific type of rental that's treated differently by the IRS—and the choice you have to make when filing this on your taxes.

▶▶ ACTION ITEMS ◀◀

○ **Not a Real Estate Investor Yet?** Consider it as an option. Not only does real estate offer great tax benefits, but it can also be a powerful wealth-building tool. However, do not just look at an investment from a tax perspective; analyze the actual investment as well.

○ **Already Investing in Real Estate?** Review the strategies in this chapter to ensure you're maximizing your tax benefits, including deductions, depreciation (such as through a cost segregation study), and potential real estate professional status.

CHAPTER 28

SHORT-TERM RENTALS

If a particular type of rental real estate deserves a chapter of its own, it's short-term rentals.

Short-term rentals are taxed differently than other rental properties, and they come with special rules and considerations you should know. But we'll keep it short and sweet.

What Is a Short-Term Rental?

Generally speaking, the IRS defines a short-term rental as a property with average rental days of *seven or fewer*. You can calculate the average rental with this simple equation:

Average rental = Total rental days / # of times rented

So, if you rent out your property 25 times during the year for a total of 150 days, your average rental would be six days (150/25), and it would qualify as a short-term rental.

Short-Term Rental Loophole

From a tax perspective, short-term rentals can be extremely attractive because you *may* be able to use losses from them to offset regular W-2 or business income. As you know from the previous chapter, rental losses are typically considered passive and can only offset passive income, but there is a short-term rental loophole to bypass this if you "materially participate."

To be considered a material participant, you need to meet *just one* of seven tests set by the IRS. In our experience, you're most likely to meet one of the following conditions:

- You participated in the activity for more than 500 hours.

- Your participation was substantially greater than all the participation in the activity of all individuals for the tax year, including individuals who didn't own interest in the activity.

- You participated in the activity for more than 100 hours during the tax year and participated at least as much as any other individual (including individuals who didn't own any interest in the activity) for the year.

If you can meet one of those tests for your short-term rental, you can use losses from that rental to offset your ordinary (W-2 or business) income. Combining this with a cost segregation study can produce some big losses upfront, and this is the power behind this strategy.

Most rental activity losses *can't* be applied against regular ordinary income, but short-term rentals are the exception **as long as you materially participate**.

Note: Be careful about using the property for personal use, as that could blow up this strategy. Working on the property would not be considered personal use if the sole purpose is related to the rental activity.

If you own or plan to own a short-term rental, it's essential to know what to expect before tax season. This type of real estate has unique advantages and disadvantages; you should factor these into your planning at every turn.

▶▶ ACTION ITEMS ◀◀

○ **Explore the Short-Term Rental Strategy:** Evaluate whether a short-term rental could be a good fit for you from both a tax and investment perspective. If so, pay close attention to the material participation requirement to ensure you qualify for the available tax benefits.

CHAPTER 29

YEAR-END TAX STRATEGIES FOR BUSINESS OWNERS

When it comes to the end of the year, there are a few strategies for cash-basis filers that can essentially shift income from one year to another. Here are the top six.

Prepayment of Certain Expenses

For cash-basis filers, prepaying some business expenses can help shift deductions into the current tax year. The IRS allows taxpayers to pay certain costs up to a year in advance and still claim the full deduction. This is particularly helpful for expenses such as:

- Payments for leasing vehicles.
- Payments for renting office space or machinery.
- Premiums for business insurance policies.

Example

Imagine your rent is $1,250 per month, and you aim to claim a $15,000 deduction in the current year. You can make a $15,000 payment on December 30 to cover the upcoming year's rent, allowing you to take a $15,000 deduction this year. Communication with your landlord about this arrangement is essential to prevent any confusion.

If your income is relatively low this year, you may want to avoid this strategy, as the deduction may be more valuable to you in the following year.

Delay Invoicing

Hold off on sending invoices to your customers, clients, or patients until after the year's end.

Why? Because individuals and insurance companies often don't make payments until they receive an invoice. By delaying invoicing until next year, you can defer the taxes associated with the income from these services.

Example

A corporate lawyer may send invoices to clients at the end of each week. However, in December, they hold off on sending any invoices. Instead, they compile these invoices and send them out during the first week of January. This shifts the income and the taxes on it to the following year.

Note: This strategy works best with clients who have a strong payment history. Prioritize reliable clients to ensure payments come through as expected in the following year.

Purchase Business Equipment

If you're already planning to invest in business equipment, completing the purchase by year-end allows you to take advantage of valuable deductions like bonus depreciation or Section 179.

These provisions allow businesses to write off a substantial portion—or even the full cost—of qualifying assets used for business purposes, including:

- Machinery and equipment.
- Office furniture such as desks and chairs.
- Technology like computers and printers.
- Specific business-use vehicles.

Now remember, we would never advise you to go out and buy something just for a tax deduction at TaxElm, but if you plan on purchasing a vehicle or equipment soon, this may be an excellent option for you.

You can read more about bonus depreciation and Section 179 expensing in **Chapter 15: Depreciation/Capitalization Policy**.

Utilize the Credit Card Trick

With a business credit card, you can deduct expenses at the time of purchase, even if you don't pay off the balance until later. This method allows last-minute deductions without requiring an immediate outlay of cash.

If your business is structured as a corporation and you use a personal credit card for these expenses, the corporation must reimburse you to qualify for the deduction. To ensure this, complete an expense report and process the reimbursement through the corporation by December 31.

Caution: Don't spend just to spend. Make sure they are necessary purchases.

Embrace Your Legal Deductions (Even If It Creates a Loss)

Tax laws are designed to support businesses through legitimate deductions, so don't shy away from claiming all deductions you're entitled to, even if it results in a net operating loss (NOL). An NOL occurs when your business expenses exceed income, which is common for new or expanding businesses and can even happen in established, profitable companies.

An NOL allows you to carry losses forward to offset future taxable income, potentially reducing taxes in more profitable years. So, rather than holding back on deductions, record every expense you can substantiate. At TaxElm, we encourage business owners to fully document and claim deductions without fear of "too many deductions."

Implement Strategies in This Book

Year-end is the perfect time to evaluate your business from every angle. Make it a habit to incorporate these strategies into your tax planning each year. When you routinely apply year-end strategies, they can become powerful tools for tax savings and improving your business's financial health.

Finally, take everything covered in this book so far and make sure these strategies are implemented in your business by December 31!

▶▶ ACTION ITEMS ◀◀

○ **Analyze Your Year-End Financials:** Review your expected income for the year and consider strategies to shift expenses into the current year if they align with your tax planning goals.

○ **Plan for Next Year:** If this year's income is lower and you expect higher earnings next year, consider holding off on certain expenses to benefit from deductions in the higher-income year.

CHAPTER 30

AFTER YEAR-END OPTIONS

A s we have stressed throughout this book, tax planning needs
to happen between January and December. Now, I know that
after reading this book you will absolutely do that, but you
may not have last year.

If that's true, you missed out on a lot of opportunities, but there
are still a few options available for newcomers. That's exactly
what we want to talk about in this chapter. Here, we'll outline tax
strategies that may be available to you come tax season for the
prior year's activity.

What Retirement Tax Strategies Are Available After Year-End?

You might be surprised to learn that some types of retirement
savings and employee benefits payments can help you cut your
tax bill even after New Year's.

TRADITIONAL IRA OR ROTH IRA

You can contribute to a traditional IRA or Roth IRA until your
tax filing date or due date. After April 15, any contributions will
count toward next year's taxes.

SEP IRA, 401(K)S AND PROFIT-SHARING

You can contribute to SEP IRAs and 401(k)s—including solo 401(k)s—until your tax filing date, including extensions. This applies to employer contributions. You can also continue making deductible profit-sharing payments to your employees after the year has ended.

Say you are a sole proprietor and want to make a SEP IRA contribution toward last year, and you have filed for and been approved for an extension on your personal return. You can make that contribution up until the date you file with a maximum or deadline of the extended due date.

Note: Employee contributions are not available after the year has ended and must be completed by December 31 of the year you're filing for.

What Business Tax Strategies Are Available After Year-End?

What about tax strategies for your other business expenses, not just your IRA payments and contributions to employee retirement accounts? Some of these are available after the calendar has turned over too, but know that they won't be as powerful as they would have been with advance planning.

COMPLETE AND ACCURATE BOOKKEEPING

If you have not yet completed your bookkeeping by the end of the year, do it now. Many business owners miss deductions they could have taken throughout the year, and you'll catch a lot more if you have a few months to work on it.

Go through all of your spending for the year with a fine-tooth comb to see if there are any deductions related to the business that can be added to bookkeeping. Think of things like:

- Internet payments.
- Cell phone plans.
- Asset purchases (laptops, tablets, smartwatches, etc.).
- Meal expenses.
- Gifts.
- Insurance premiums.
- Office expenses/supplies.
- Travel expenses.
- And more.

Essentially, take the time now to see if there were business expenses you may have paid personally that can be switched over and included in your business bookkeeping—and, thus, your tax return. In the future, you'll know to pay these as business expenses from the start for cleaner books and more savings.

HOME OFFICE DEDUCTION

Do not be afraid to take a valid home office deduction. Somewhere along the line, accountants tried to scare business owners with this one, but it is a completely legal deduction that every business owner should be taking advantage of.

AUTOMOBILE EXPENSES

Vehicle purchases would need to be made before December 31 to be included in next year's taxes and bookkeeping, but this doesn't apply to mileage. A personal vehicle used for business at year-end should be considered, and its mileage should be calculated for your tax filing.

COST SEGREGATION STUDY

After the tax year has ended, rental property owners can still consider conducting cost segregation studies. This financial analysis allows them to accelerate depreciation deductions on their property, which can lead to significant tax savings. Revisit **Chapter 27: Real Estate Taxes** for more on this topic.

What Other Tax Strategies Are Available After Year-End?

To keep reducing your tax bill after the year has ended, but before you file, look to your specialized savings accounts. Savings can be found with both HSAs and Coverdell IRAs.

HSAS

As if this type of account needed another reason for us to get excited about it, you can contribute to your HSA until your tax filing due date (April 15). Keep adding to your medical nest egg if you have the means! Put that end-of-year bonus or funds you've squirreled away to good use.

COVERDELL IRA

A Coverdell IRA is an IRA designed specifically for education savings. You do not get a tax deduction for this one, but you can make tax-free withdrawals from it for qualified education expenses. This applies to both principal and earnings. You can also contribute to a Coverdell IRA until your tax filing due date (April 15).

Calendar Deadlines for In-Season Tax Saving Strategies

Of course, the best tax savings strategies are those you plan and prepare for. Always be mindful of tax deadlines on the calendar and do your best to get ready for them long before the year is over. Here are the two due dates to remember and the strategies they apply to.

- **April 15 or the filing date (if earlier)**
    ○ Traditional or Roth IRAs.
    ○ HSAs.
    ○ Coverdell IRAs.
- **September 15 (S-corp and Partnerships), October 15, or the filing date (if earlier)**
    ○ Employer contributions to SEP IRAs, solo 401(k)s, 401(k)s, profit-sharing, etc.
    ○ Business strategies.

Hopefully, this gives you a few last-minute options to save on your taxes even if you weren't doing everything outlined in this book to gear up for them. And if you are stuck with a big tax bill this year, let this serve as a reminder to get on top of tax planning now so you can ensure you have more strategies available next time—especially the ones you need to do before year-end to qualify!

▶▶ ACTION ITEMS ◀◀

○ **Options Still Available:** Even if tax planning slipped to the back burner until after year-end, there are still options you can take advantage of. Review the strategies here and implement those that align with your goals.

○ **Plan for Next Year:** Let this chapter be a reminder to start planning earlier next year to maximize your tax-saving opportunities.

CHAPTER 31

SUCCESSION PLANNING AND EXIT STRATEGIES

I f you are reading this book, you are likely not thinking about selling your business at the moment, but the time will come when you are ready to move on. You may be exiting to retire and sail off in the sunset, or you may be excited to start the next best thing. Either way, whether that time is 10 months or 10 years down the road, it is something you should be thinking about now.

In order to have a successful business transition, there are a lot of decisions you need to make and there are a lot of things you can do ahead of time to make the process smooth. At TaxElm, we have found that members who think about exiting at least three years prior to the actual event end up with a higher sale price and fewer taxes on the exit. Even if you are a business owner just starting, you should be thinking about how to set up and grow your business for an eventual exit sometime down the road.

Key Steps in Succession Planning

Every business's succession will look different, but many will follow this basic structure.

- **Identify potential successors.** Successors could be family members, current employees, or external candidates you think have what it takes to help your business thrive without you.

- **Assess and develop skills.** Once you've identified potential successors, assess their current skills and develop a plan to fill any gaps. Make sure they're willing and able to start learning now.

- **Create a transition plan.** Document how and when the transfer of leadership and responsibilities will occur. The clearer, the better.

- **Communicate the plan.** Ensure all stakeholders are aware of the succession plan to avoid confusion and conflict.

Business Exit Strategies

A pre-thought-out exit strategy is vital for a successful transition. You can find stories in every city about a business sale gone wrong; you don't want to be just another story in your city. Some exit options include:

- **Selling the business:** This can be to a current employee, someone from the outside, an existing partner, or even private equity.

- **Passing it to the family:** This is often your children, but it could be any family member. It may be done with the help of a trust or gradual gifting.

- **Liquidation:** If no successor is identified, the business assets are usually sold alone, and the business closes its doors.

When transferring or selling a business, the tax implications are significant and will impact the net proceeds you receive from the sale.

Note: The best way to make your business more valuable is to put systems in place that allow it to run without you. When a potential buyer is looking to purchase a business, having the owner be a necessity for the business to run smoothly lowers its value.

Tax Considerations for Succession

Regardless of the exit strategy that you eventually decide upon, you want to consider the tax implications and plan for them ahead of time.

- **Capital gains tax:** This will make up the bulk of the taxes you'll be responsible for paying upon the sale of your business.

- **Estate taxes:** If you decide to pass your business to your heirs, estate taxes may apply, depending on the value of the business and the applicable tax laws at that time.

- **Gift taxes:** If you are transferring ownership through gifting, be aware of the gift tax rules and annual exemptions.

Strategies To Minimize Tax Liabilities

No matter how you plan your succession, be smart about it. Consider these tax planning strategies and which ones may apply to your situation down the road.

- **Installment sale:** Spreading the receipt of

proceeds over several years can reduce your tax burden by spreading out the capital gains.

- **Gifting shares:** Gradually gifting shares to heirs can let you take advantage of annual gift tax exclusions and reduce estate taxes.

- **Charitable trusts:** Transferring a portion of the business to a charitable trust can provide tax benefits while supporting a good cause.

- **Employee Stock Ownership Plan (ESOP):** Selling your business to employees through an ESOP can provide tax advantages and motivate employees to perform by giving them a stake in the business's future.

- **1031 exchange (real estate):** This strategy allows you to reinvest the proceeds from the sale of real estate into a new property of like kind and defer all capital gains taxes. The IRS has strict rules around these and you need to ensure this decision is made prior to the sale. At TaxElm, we recommend working with a professional to ensure the entire process is followed correctly.

ADVANCED STRATEGIES

If you are looking at a potential gain of $500,000 or more, you will want to start digging into some more advanced strategies to help with the tax burden. At TaxElm, we can't stress enough the importance of working with a qualified professional well in advance of your sale.

Succession planning and a well thought out exit strategy are likely not something that is top of mind. Use this chapter as a reminder that anything can happen at any time, and having a rough plan can never hurt. If you are at a point where an exit is expected within the next five years, take the time now to lay out your plan and be best prepared so you can focus on a smooth transition with a lower tax hit.

SMALL BUSINESS TAX SAVINGS **HANDBOOK**

▶▶ ACTION ITEMS ◀◀

○ **Consult a Professional:** If you're planning to sell an asset with a significant capital gain, consult a tax professional before completing the sale to develop a strategy for minimizing taxes.

○ **Become an Absentee Business Owner:** The more your business can run without you, the more valuable your business will be. This is the importance of developing a management team or key employee that is engulfed in the day-to-day operations of your business. This doesn't have to happen overnight but can always be a work in progress.

CHAPTER 32

AUDIT-PROOF GUIDE

We've talked about ways to legally save on your taxes throughout this entire book. But if you're still nervous about the possibility of an IRS audit and how to handle one should it ever happen to you, think of this chapter as an audit-proof guide.

A lot of this section will be reviewing concepts and strategies we've already gone over. To help you out, we'll tell you exactly which chapters to go back to if you need to revisit something.

Remember the Burden of Proof

The burden of proof is on the taxpayer. This is just the way these things work.

With the topic of taxes comes many business owners' biggest fear: the dreaded audit. Business owners are so afraid of an IRS audit that they let it impact many areas of their lives and often end up paying more in taxes than necessary.

But you don't need to pay more to avoid being audited. You just need to be mindful of the burden of proof—which is on *you*.

The IRS website says:

"The responsibility to prove entries, deductions, and statements made on your tax returns is known as the burden of proof. You must be able to prove (substantiate) certain elements of expenses to deduct them. Generally, taxpayers meet their burden of proof by having the information and receipts (where needed) for the expenses. You should keep adequate records to prove your expenses or have sufficient evidence that will support your own statement. You generally must have documentary evidence, such as receipts, canceled checks, or bills, to support your expenses. Additional evidence is required for travel, entertainment, gifts, and auto expenses."

This is why it's so important to take your time to do your taxes right. Avoiding an audit is about proving your deductions so you can protect yourself, feel confident, and stress less.

Let's start with best practices for audit-proofing your taxes.

Best Practices

We discussed best practices for tax planning in **Chapter 3: Starting a Business - Saving and Planning for Taxes** and gave five rules you should always follow to avoid trouble. We'll review them here.

- **Take bookkeeping seriously.** Do it immediately, do it often, and use it to better your business.

- **Keep separate bank accounts.** No personal expenses should go on the business account, and no business expenses should go on a personal account.

- **Avoid commingling.** Prevent mistakes by staying

organized (but record them when they do happen).

- **Keep your receipts.** This is critical for effective record-keeping.
- **Ditch the cash.** Other payment methods, like credit cards, are safer and easier to track.

Your chances of being audited are actually pretty low, but they're even lower when you follow these rules year in and year out.

Red Flags

The IRS is always on the lookout for red flags. If they find them, this is when you need to worry about an audit coming your way. Here are some tips for avoiding suspicion.

Large Personal Deductions

The IRS may become suspicious of large deductions disproportionate to income. The agency uses tables to determine how much is too much for deductions at each income bracket and can and will call out discrepancies. If, for example, it looks like you're far too charitable for someone with your reported income, your return may get flagged.

Don't get greedy with the personal deductions.

Excessive Business Deductions

The IRS is tough on business owners who mix business and personal expenses, which usually manifests as too many business deductions. At TaxElm, we strongly encourage clients to take advantage of available deductions without being too liberal with business write-offs.

Expenses should make sense based on your income level and be ordinary and necessary for your business. If there's any doubt in your mind about a business expense, use personal funds.

Round Numbers

You should never round up or average numbers on your tax return. Nice, round numbers are not common, so using these is a red flag. If, for example, your sales are $232,098.29 in a given year, you should not round down to $232,000. Keep it precise.

Late and Paper Returns

The IRS hates late returns and isn't keen on paper returns either. If you need more time, file for an extension rather than submit late. And if you have your return ready in time but can't pay what you owe, you should still file by the deadline.

All too often, business owners prepare their taxes and see an amount due they can't afford, so they submit late. This leads to penalties and problems. Instead, set up a payment plan to take care of your balance.

Historically, paper tax returns have been audited at a higher rate than electronic returns because they more often contain errors. Take advantage of the convenience and safety of electronic filing, which also offers faster processing times and helps to save trees!

Note: If you have independent contractors or employees, be sure to issue and file your 1099s and W-2s in January. Collect a W-9 from your contractors before you pay them so you have the required information on file.

Proving Expenses

Chapter 13: Maximizing Deductions goes into detail about how to make your deductible expenses airtight. Here, we'll review what's required as proof for every expense and a few of the top expense categories with special requirements.

REQUIREMENTS

To prove an expense, you need:

- A receipt or invoice.
- Proof of payment (bank or credit card statement).

Here's what each of these should include, as well as how to store them:

RECEIPT OR INVOICE

A receipt or an invoice outlines exactly what you purchase. Itemized receipts break everything down into as much detail as possible, so they're always great to have when you can get them.
On every receipt, write the following:

- **Who:** List who was involved in the expense.
- **What:** List what was purchased.
- **Where:** List where the purchase occurred.
- **When:** List the date, time, and duration of the purchase.
- **Why:** Provide a brief outline of the business purpose.

Example

You go to lunch at Moe's Steakhouse with a potential client, Bob. The receipt you get from the restaurant is itemized, showing exactly what you two ordered. It shows the restaurant name (where) and a time stamp (when) already. You add, by writing directly on the receipt, that you met with Bob (who) to discuss bringing his business over to yours (why).

PROOF OF PAYMENT

Proof of payment simply shows that you paid for an item. This is usually straightforward, as expenses often come directly from your business bank account or credit card. You can use bank statements, credit card statements, or even canceled checks as proof.

This item just prevents people from claiming deductions for expenses that aren't their own by requiring people to match their expenses to their payments.

STORAGE

We always recommend keeping your receipts and proof of purchase documents in a digital file. This allows for easier, faster sorting and advanced organization.

AUTOMOBILE EXPENSES

Automobile expenses require a little more proof than many other deductions.

In **Chapter 18: Automobile Expenses**, we share tips for keeping a mileage log and tracking the business purpose for your miles. Here's a brief review of this concept:

MILEAGE LOGS

The IRS requires proof of business miles and offers the following options for keeping mileage logs:

- **Mileage log for every day of the year.**
- **Three-month sample.**

BUSINESS PURPOSE

You'll recall that you also need to prove the business purpose of your miles. To do this, just record the purpose of your business miles in your appointment book so you can trace all expenses back to the source. And if you have other expenses to support your purpose, like Starbucks stops or meetings with clients, keep records of these with your miles too.

Note: Distinguish between business and personal miles. Odometer readings are helpful.

EMPLOYEE EXPENSES

For all payments you make to employees when hiring and paying them, you'll need to provide proof that these are viable business expenses. To do this, you'll keep the following documents:

- Timesheets (date, description, and hours).
- Employee agreements/job descriptions.
- Reasonable wage support.
- Proof of payments.
- Tax payments.
- Form filings.

For more information about employees and independent contractors, see **Chapter 8: Hiring Employees**.

TRAVEL EXPENSES

Revisit **Chapter 17: Meals and Travel Expenses** for an in-depth guide to travel deductions and how to take them.

Whenever you travel for business, you should have a day-to-day log that tracks the business purpose and activity for the entire trip to prove its deductibility. If you have personal days in there, ensure that this is tracked properly.

- Where are you traveling to and why?
- Who are you meeting with, and where are you meeting them?
- How much time did you spend on business for each day?

The items we discussed in the receipts section will help with a lot of these as well.

Note: Although receipts are technically not required for automobile or travel expenses less than $75, we recommend keeping them anyway. They help provide strong evidence and show the IRS that you're on top of things.

ASSET PURCHASES

Keep as much documentation as possible for asset purchases that will depreciate. Things like:

- Bills of sale.
- Loan agreements (if necessary).
- Pictures of the asset.
- Receipts/invoices/proof of payments.

See **Chapter 13: Maximizing Deductions** and **Chapter 15: Depreciation/Capitalization Policy** for more on depreciation.

AGREEMENTS

Have all agreements related to your business on file while they are active. Often, these help defend expenses and can serve as part of your proof. Examples include:

- Contracts.
- Rental agreements.
- Lease agreements.
- Consulting agreements.
- Contractor agreements.
- Joint venture agreements.

Avoiding an IRS audit isn't about luck. It's about doing things properly with the right records, justifications, and deductions at every turn.

Another key thing to understand is that as long as you have all of the documentation, support, proof, backup, etc., even if you happen to be selected for an audit, you have nothing to worry about. The IRS will review your items and move on!

▶▶ ACTION ITEMS ◀◀

○ **Protect Yourself:** Put the work in on the front end to ensure you have everything you need to defend the deductions you are taking.

○ **Sleep Easy:** As long as you have solid documentation, you have nothing to worry about. If the IRS comes knocking, you have everything readily on hand to submit and move on.

○ **If You Get Audited:** Don't panic. Gather your documents, provide what is requested, and seek a tax resolution expert if needed.

CHAPTER 33

TAX PLANNING STRATEGIES FOR W-2 EMPLOYEES

What tax strategies are available for W-2 employees?

This is a great question, and the answer is many of the same strategies available for business owners! Since we've been sharing strategies for business owners throughout this book, a lot of this chapter will be revisiting concepts we've already covered, including:

- Retirement plans.
- Health savings accounts.
- Rental properties.
- And more.

This time around, we'll provide tips for executing these strategies from a personal perspective.

We want to make a quick note that if you make more than $400,000 per year, you'll want to look into more advanced strategies in addition to what we're going to talk about here.

Retirement for W-2 Employees

First things first, let's talk about retirement options many employers offer. This includes SIMPLE IRAs, 401(k) plans, and 403(b) plans. Depending on your plan, you will make pre-tax contributions and potentially after-tax (Roth) contributions. There are pros and cons to both.

Pre-Tax Contributions

Pre-tax contributions you make to a retirement plan reduce your taxable income, saving you money. But you pay taxes when making withdrawals.

Say you're in the 24% tax bracket and contribute $10,000 into your pre-tax retirement account. In this instance, you're saving $2,400 in taxes that year but will pay taxes later on. Think of this strategy as a tax deferral. Get a tax break today and pay taxes later.

After-Tax Contributions (Roth)

Roth contributions you make to a retirement plan do *not* reduce your taxable income. And when you remove funds, you aren't taxed. With this plan, you get a tax benefit later instead of today and pay taxes on your contributions, not withdrawals.

Many people do a combination of the two and contribute to both a pre-tax and an after-tax retirement plan.

Employer Matching

We highly recommend that W-2 employees fully utilize matches their company offers. This is free money for your retirement that your company will provide.

Outside Plans

Aside from your company retirement plan, you can also look at a traditional or Roth IRA. There are income limits and phase-out ranges to be mindful of for each, but these can help supplement your retirement savings.

Tax planning for retirement comes down to whether you want to have pre-tax or after-tax contributions (or some mixture of the two). And if you can use employer matches, do it.

HSAs for W-2 Employees

As we covered in **Chapter 23: Health Savings Accounts (HSAs)**, an HSA is a type of savings account that can be used for medical expenses. We recommend these to both W-2 employees and business owners who qualify because:

- You get a tax deduction for contributions.
- Withdrawals are tax-free when used for qualified medical expenses.
- Interest/earnings are not taxed.

This is a powerful savings vehicle that lets you win when putting money in and taking it out, and everyone should max out their HSAs every year if they can. To be eligible to open an HSA, you need a high-deductible health plan.

Note: Be aware of annual contribution limits for these accounts.

WHAT ABOUT FLEXIBLE SPENDING ACCOUNTS?

If you don't qualify for an HSA, consider an FSA.

A flexible spending account (FSA) allows you to pay for certain items with pre-tax money. You get a tax deduction for the contribution and tax-free withdrawals for qualifying expenses.

The biggest downside is that these accounts are "use it or lose it," meaning funds don't roll over.

Rental Properties for W-2 Employees

We talked about how rental properties can help owners save on taxes while growing their wealth in detail in **Chapter 27: Real Estate Taxes**. And we want to talk about it again here.

Rentals often produce losses in the early years because of depreciation and operating costs. However, you usually can't use passive losses (rental activity) to offset W-2 income. So why are we telling you about rental properties as a W-2 tax strategy? Because passive losses can be carried forward to offset passive income in the future. Also, there are a few strategies that do let you use rental losses to offset W-2 income.

Strategies like:

- **Being an active investor.** This status allows you to claim up to $25,000 in rental losses if you actively participate in managing it.

- **Being a real estate professional.** This status lets you fully deduct passive losses against your W-2 income. But there are a handful of strict requirements to meet.

- **Having a short-term rental.** If your average rental is seven days or fewer and you materially participate in managing the property, you can use losses to offset your W-2 income.

Again, head back to **Chapter 27: Real Estate Taxes** for a deeper look at each of these strategies.

Starting a Side Business

Starting a business is the easiest way to turn after-tax spending into pre-tax spending. As a business owner, you can deduct a lot of your everyday spending that you wouldn't be able to deduct as a W-2 employee alone.

Is there a side business you could start? It doesn't have to be a full-time gig or replace your W-2. If you're already interested in starting one, this could be another reason to do it.

Other Tax Planning Strategies Available for W-2 Employees

But wait, there's more. Here are a couple of other strategies you can use when tax planning to pay less in taxes.

Itemized Deductions vs. Standard Deduction

You have the option to either claim the standard deduction or itemize your deductions, depending on which provides a greater benefit. If your itemized deductions are nearly equal to your standard deduction, you might want to consider "bunching" your itemized deductions into a single year to maximize their value.

Itemized deductions include:

- Medical and dental expenses.
- State and local taxes.
- Mortgage interest.
- Charitable contributions.

College Savings

You can contribute to a 529 plan for college savings. There is no federal deduction for this contribution, but your state may offer a tax deduction.

For you W-2 employees out there, I hope these tips have been helpful and given you some ideas for planning. This is the last topic we're going to cover in our book, so head over to the next chapter for our best attempt at wrapping up the vast and exciting topic of tax planning!

▶▶ ACTION ITEMS ◀◀

○ **Don't Wave the White Flag:** As a W2 employee, your tax saving options are limited, but it doesn't mean you do not have any available. Utilize the incentives the government has given you to your full advantage.

○ **Consider a Side Business or Real Estate Investment:** Explore opportunities to start a side business or invest in real estate, both of which offer unique tax advantages beyond W-2 income.

CHAPTER 34

SUMMARY

Congratulations! If you have made it this far, you are on your way to paying the least amount in taxes legally possible. With that being said, this is just the start of your journey.

Learning these tax strategies is great, but it does not automatically lead to tax savings. The most important part is *implementation*. Learning and then using tax strategies is what truly leads to you paying less at tax time.

Always Take Advantage of Incentives

I hope this book has opened up the door to a new way of thinking. The government's way of getting things they want is to provide incentives. They provide incentives to business owners so they can hire employees, innovate, grow the economy, contribute to the economy, and so much more. The government provides incentives to rental property owners to provide housing, stimulate the economy, and so much more.

Unfortunately, the government does not implement these incentives for you. It does not put them on billboards across the country. It is your job as a taxpayer to understand the incentives offered to you and use them to your advantage.

Use this book as your guide moving forward. Not everything will be relevant to you at all times. You may come back to certain chapters down the road or re-read the entire book every year as a refresher on what is available to you. Just remember, learning is simply the first step in the process; now, you need to go out and implement the items you have learned!

Resources

To help you take that next step, we have plenty of resources that you can check out:

- **Book updates:** Tax law is constantly changing, and we'll share any changes that affect the contents of this book. Go to the link below for updates!
  - ° http://updates.taxsavingsbook.com/
- **Small Business Tax Savings Podcast:** Every week, we do a new episode focused on various tax strategies. You can find our podcast on any platform you use. Subscribe and tune in each week, or go to the link below to start listening.
  - ° www.TaxSavingsPodcast.com
- **Small Business Tax Savings TV:** With this channel, we provide educational content on tax-related topics, offering viewers tips and strategies to reduce their tax liabilities and maximize their savings. The channel features a variety of videos aimed at helping individuals and businesses understand and navigate the complexities of tax laws and regulations. Subscribe and get access to each new video we launch.
  - ° www.TaxSavingsTV.com

- **TaxElm:** TaxElm is your ultimate resource for eliminating taxes and growing your wealth. With features like a custom tax plan, unlimited access to our team of tax experts, live consultations, tax return reviews, monthly webinars, partner discounts, and a rich learning center, TaxElm is designed to help you pay less in taxes every year while expanding your business and personal wealth. If you are looking for a tax strategist on your team to help knock out the implementation piece of tax planning, this is your resource.
  - ° www.TaxElm.com

Whatever direction you want to go next in this tax savings journey, we have an option for you. Here's to paying the least amount in taxes legally possible!

▶▶ ACTION ITEMS ◀◀

◯ Visit the **Small Business Tax Savings Handbook** Updates Page

◯ Subscribe to the **Small Business Tax Savings Podcast**

◯ Subscribe to **Small Business Tax Savings TV** on YouTube

◯ Explore **TaxElm**

TAXELM

YOUR RESOURCE FOR

ELIMINATING TAX & GROWING YOUR WEALTH

Tax Savings Blueprint & TrainingLibrary

Unlimited Access to Tax Experts

Annual Comprehensive Consultation

Annual Tax Return Review

Monthly Webinars & Training

Partner Directory and Discounts

Learn more at:

www.TaxElm.com

Book Specific Resources

Book Website:

www.TaxSavingsBook.com

Access Book Updates:

http://updates.taxsavingsbook.com

Thank You for Reading!

I hope you found this book valuable in helping you maximize tax savings and grow your business. Your feedback means a lot to me, and I'd love to hear what you think!

If you enjoyed this book or found it helpful, please consider leaving a review wherever you purchased it.

Your review not only helps other business owners discover these strategies but also allows me to keep improving and sharing insights that matter most to you.

Thank you for your support and for being part of this journey to financial success and tax minimization!